The Human Genome

by Megan Mitchell

Cavendish
Square

New York

Published in 2017 by Cavendish Square Publishing, LLC
243 5th Avenue, Suite 136, New York, NY 10016

Website: cavendishsq.com

This publication represents the opinions and views of the author based on his or her
personal experience, knowledge, and research. The information in this book serves as a general
guide only. The author and publisher have used their best efforts in preparing this book and
disclaim liability rising directly or indirectly from the use and application of this book.

CPSIA Compliance Information: Batch #CS16CSQ

All websites were available and accurate when this book was sent to press.

Library of Congress Cataloging-in-Publication Data

Names: Mitchell, Megan.
Title: The human genome / Megan Mitchell.
Description: New York : Cavendish Square Publishing, [2017] | Series:
Great   discoveries in science | Includes bibliographical references and index.
Identifiers: LCCN 2016002177 (print) | LCCN 2016011156 (ebook) |
ISBN 9781502619532 (library bound) | ISBN 9781502619549 (ebook)
Subjects: LCSH: Human genome. | Genetics.
Classification: LCC QH437 .M58 2017 (print) | LCC QH437 (ebook) |
DDC 576.5--dc23
LC record available at http://lccn.loc.gov/2016002177 Library of Congress

Editorial Director: David McNamara
Editor: Leah Tallon
Copy Editor: Michele Suchomel-Casey
Art Director: Jeffrey Talbot
Designer: Joseph Macri and Lindsey Auten
Production Assistant: Karol Szymczuk
Photo Research: J8 Media

The photographs in this book are used by permission and through the courtesy of: Andrew Brookes/Getty
Images, cover; Karen Kasmauski/Science Faction/Getty Images, 4; Festa/Shutterstock.com, 8; Spencer Sutton/
Science Source/Getty Images, 11; Visuals Unlimited, Inc./Solvin Zankl/Getty Images, 14; © blickwinkel/Alamy
Stock Photo, 15; Source - Science/Science Source/Getty Images, 16; Universal History Archive/UIG via Getty
Images, 18; © Universal Images Group North America LLC/Alamy Stock Photo, 20; Photo Researchers/Science
Source/Getty Image, 28; Pbroks13/File:Punnett Square.svg/Wikimedia Commons, 34; Unknown/File:Ishihara
9.png/Wikimedia Commons, 37; NCI/File:Point Mutation.jpg/Wikimedia Commons, 39; Alila Medical Media/
Shutetrstock.com, 41; Bill Clark/CQ Roll Call/Getty Images, 46; Twaanders17/File:Drosophila Gene Linkage Map.
svg/Wikimedia Commons, 49; SSPL/Getty Images, 51; Gio.tto/Shutterstock.com, 52; ullstein bild/ullstein bild
via Getty Images, 53; Christopher Halloran/Shutterstock.com, 58; © Agencja Fotograficzna Caro/Alamy Stock
Photo, 59; Visuals Unlimited, Inc./Heiti Paves/Getty Images, 64; © Martin Shields/Alamy Stock Photo, 69; BSIP/
UIG/Getty Images, 71; Rita Maas/The Image Bank/Getty Images, 75; Blamb/Shutterstock.com, 77; Stegerphoto/
Photolibrary/Getty Images, 87; Serg64/Shutterstock.com, 88; Mark Wilson/Newsmakers/Getty Images, 90;
AEKLAK/Shutterstock.com, 93; Juan Gaertner/Shutterstock.com, 96; sciencepics/Shutterstock.com, 100.

Printed in the United States of America

Contents

Dolly the sheep, the first successfully cloned mammal, lived for six years and gave birth to six lambs. She now resides at the National Museum of Scotland.

Introduction

Dolly the sheep lived a calm and uneventful life. She gave birth to six lambs, including a set of twins and one set of triplets. She lived seven years before passing away from illness. Although she lived an ordinary life, Dolly is one of the most well-known and important animals to scientific research. She was born a healthy lamb on July 5, 1996. The sheep that gave birth to Dolly was not her biological mother. In fact, Dolly did not have a biological parent as typically defined. Instead, she began her life in a test tube. Dolly was the first mammal to be cloned from an adult body cell. The process of cloning involves removing the instructions from one cell and implanting them into a reproductive cell. The cell is then moved to a surrogate. The plant or animal that is born is an exact duplicate of the original organism. Dolly's birth was amazing because it was the first successful transfer of instructions from an adult sheep. By the time an organism reaches adulthood, most cells in its body only use information necessary to their particular function. Heart cells, for example, do not need all the same instructions to operate as skin cells. Dolly was the only successful birth out of 237 attempts to transfer information from an adult cell.

After the announcement of Dolly's birth, controversy surrounding scientific advances such as cloning and stem cell research quickly moved into the public eye. Rarely had a scientific discovery elicited such a divided and heated response. Soon, a massive public debate erupted between politicians, religious leaders, scientists, educators, and the general public, who either vocally supported or opposed human interference in biology.

The field of biology and, in particular, genetics is rapidly changing. After Dolly's successful birth, scientists have gone on to clone many more mammalian species, including horses, dogs, and cats. Modern experiments have produced even more sophisticated results. Hybrid animals, such as the beefalo, combine two different organisms, a cow and a buffalo, into a new type of animal. Scientists have created animals, like kittens or fish, that glow in the dark while other animals have been altered to produce materials for humans.

As a result of these scientific advances, there are new developments and innovations in medicine and health care. Using stem cells, scientists can grow organs, like lungs and hearts, in the laboratory. Stem cells are found in many organisms. They are undifferentiated, or not yet a particular type of cell, such as a fat cell, with a particular function. In normal development, they eventually build the tissue and organs of animals and the structures in plants. This means stem cell research carries the potential for allowing scientists and doctors to replace damaged cells, tissue, and organs in human beings.

Modern-day research is possible because of many decades of scientific study. As new discoveries and treatments develop, there continues to be a debate on the appropriate uses of technology. Is it acceptable for scientists to perform experiments and alter organisms simply because they can? Should research be used only to treat disease and illness or can it create plants that grow faster and animals with special abilities, or even alter human traits such as intelligence or personality? Dolly was only one success in a long line of cloning experiments. However, her birth represented a turning point in the scientific community.

Biological investigation and experimentation are polarizing topics in society. New research has the potential to improve the quality of life for humans and other species. However, as scientists learn more about the intricate workings of the human body, there is an equal concern for how far science should go to modify nature.

Like Dolly the sheep, the discovery of the human genome altered the future of medicinal, agricultural, and scientific research. Beginning in the mid-1800s with a scientist named Gregor Mendel, this book traces the discovery of the genetic code found in all living things while providing background on biological terms and processes necessary to understanding the science behind the exploration and discovery of the human genome. We'll explore several major scientists involved in the breakthrough, detailing the entire Human Genome Project from before its launch in 1990 to its completion in 2003, before examining the impact of the discovery of the human genome on more recent scientific advancements such as GMO technology, gene therapy, and cancer research.

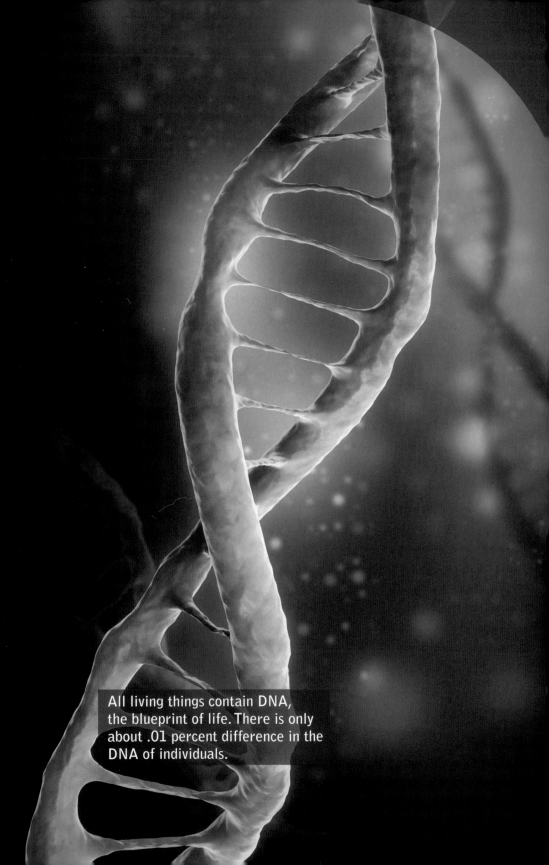
All living things contain DNA, the blueprint of life. There is only about .01 percent difference in the DNA of individuals.

CHAPTER 1

The Problem of Mapping Human Genetic Code

For many centuries, humans understood that they could control the traits of plants and animals. Breeding organisms with specific traits meant that their offspring would also have those traits. Humans controlled the characteristics of dogs, for instance, by selecting animals with desired traits and breeding them for more than fourteen thousand years. There are more than four hundred distinct breeds of dogs as a result of human intervention. Each of these diverse breeds, whether Labradors or Chihuahuas, developed by the careful selection of desired traits.

Farmers controlled the selection of desired traits for their crops and animals. If a farmer wanted cows with thick hides to tolerate harsh winters, he or she would choose a bull and a cow with thick hides to mate. Their calves would have thick, warm hides. Many of the fruits found in modern grocery stores do not resemble fruits in the wild as farmers domesticated crops to have helpful, or desirable, traits.

At the beginning of the nineteenth century, however, there were no exact rules that explained the transmission of traits from one generation to the next. Scientists knew that parents passed traits to their offspring. They also understood that some characteristics were more likely to appear in the offspring than others. There was evidence that certain traits would disappear and show up in later generations. However, there were no explanations for this aside from human intervention.

GREGOR MENDEL

In the 1850s, Gregor Mendel, a monk, addressed the mystery of trait **inheritance**. Why did offspring resemble their parents? Why, in some cases, did offspring appear to have major differences from their parents? Where did those traits go?

Mendel conducted multiple experiments to answer these questions. He investigated the inheritance of traits in pea plants. He chose to study pea plants because they grow quickly and have traits that are easy to observe, such as seed color and texture. Pea plants produce yellow or green seeds. Also, they can produce wrinkled or smooth seeds. Both of these are traits that are passed down from one generation to the next. Mendel was interested in learning why more of his plants had yellow, smooth seeds. In his first round of experiments, he cross-pollinated a pea plant with yellow seeds with a plant with only green seeds. Much to his surprise, all of the descendent plants had yellow seeds. The green seed trait disappeared. He then bred two of the yellow offspring. About 75 percent of the third generation had yellow seeds and about 25 percent had green seeds. Why did the green trait disappear in the first generation and reappear in the next? He continued breeding successive generations of pea plants. In each generation, the ratio of yellow seeds to green seeds remained fairly consistent. About three-quarters of the offspring had the yellow seed trait, and a smaller percentage, about one-quarter, had green seeds. The results were similar with seed texture: about 75 percent of plants had smooth seeds while only 25 percent had wrinkled seeds. Even when Mendel cross-pollinated plants with different combinations of traits, these ratios remained constant.

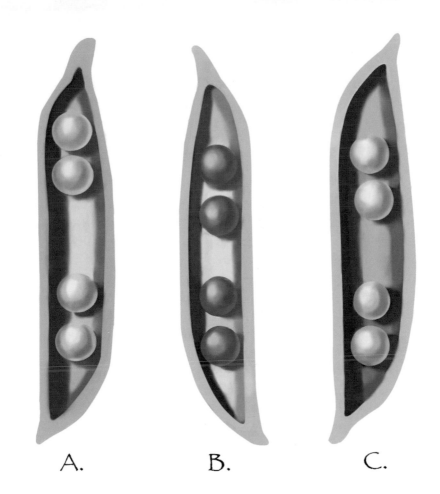

A.

B.

C.

D.

Pea plants are thought to have originated in middle Asia over three thousand years ago. Their seeds come in a variety of colors including yellow and green.

Mendel used these results to develop several important rules for how organisms acquire traits from their parents. This field of scientific study is called **heredity**.

Mendel's Laws of Heredity

Gregor Mendel's experiments demonstrated rules for heredity. First, his experiments showed that traits are inherited as a single trait, such as seed color or texture. These traits come in pairs, one from each parent. The rule of independent inheritance is called the law of segregation.

The second law of heredity is the law of dominance. Although an organism inherits a pair of traits from its parents, it will express the **dominant** trait. One trait can mask the other as with the yellow seed color over the green seed color. Mendel called such a trait "dominant." Even if a trait does not appear in the first generation, it will be passed down and may appear in later generations. Mendel coined the term "**recessive**" to describe masked traits like green seed color.

Lastly, traits are inherited independently, meaning the inheritance of one trait will not affect the inheritance of other characteristics. For instance, the trait of eye color does not influence inherited hair color. This rule is called the law of independent assortment.

These laws apply to all organisms. In humans, for example, the trait for dimples is dominant. Babies inherit two possibilities from their parents. If a man with dimples has a child with a woman with no dimples, the child will inherit the dominant trait. However, the recessive trait, no dimples, does not disappear. It is passed down and potentially expressed in later generations.

Mendel's experiments and laws of heredity were an incredible scientific breakthrough. Before his research, the prediction of inherited traits was based on guessing and superstition. Mendel demonstrated that the inheritance of traits is a measurable, predictable pattern. Scientists of the time still did not understand the exact mechanism for how traits were passed down from one generation to the next.

Unfortunately, Gregor Mendel did not receive recognition during his lifetime. Three decades later, at the beginning of the twentieth century, scientists rediscovered his experiments, ushering in what is now called the "Age of **Genetics**."

FREDERICH MIESCHER and DEOXYRIBONUCLEIC ACID

While Mendel conducted his pea plant experiments, another scientist, Frederich Miescher, made an incredible discovery. A contemporary of Gregor Mendel, Frederich Miescher is credited with first identifying **deoxyribonucleic acid**, or DNA. Miescher observed DNA, which he called "nuclein," in the **nucleus** of a white blood cell. The nucleus is the control center for a cell. He theorized that this new molecule was linked to the nucleus' vital function. He later observed the same material in other organisms' cells. Although, in this time, the exact structure of DNA was unknown, scientists now know that it is the genetic blueprint for all living things.

THOMAS MORGAN and the FLY ROOM

Mendel published his pea plant experiments in 1865. Despite the importance of his work, many questions were still unanswered. How were different parental versions passed to offspring? What determined the expression of traits in offspring? In 1908, Thomas Morgan, a scientist and professor, studied the underlying mechanisms of Mendel's heredity laws. To answer these questions, Morgan needed to observe an organism that quickly reproduced. He designed an experiment that would allow him to observe the inheritance of traits in a setting with little human influence.

Fruit flies' life span is typically forty to fifty days. A single female can lay up to five hundred eggs during her short life.

At Columbia University, Morgan established a famous laboratory, called the Fly Room, where he and a research team observed generation after generation of fruit flies. Fruit flies, *Drosophila melanogaster*, were the perfect specimens for his experiment because they reproduced quickly. The research team focused on the observable trait of eye color. The dominant eye color in fruit flies is white. Twenty generations of parents with white eyes yielded offspring with white eyes. However, in the twenty-first generation, a male fly with red eyes was born. The male with the recessive red eye trait followed the laws of heredity. The fly inherited a possibility for eye color from each parent. While red eyes were not present in the first twenty generations, the trait was still passed down.

Because Morgan allowed the reproduction to occur naturally, this surprising result indicated that Mendel's rules were part of a natural, biological process. Morgan and his team determined that traits are passed down on specific pieces

of DNA called **genes**. The term "gene" had been in use since 1909, but Morgan's fruit fly research demonstrated that certain genes were linked with certain traits. These results led to the chromosomal theory of inheritance. If Gregor Mendel was responsible for discovering the instruction manual of heredity, Thomas Morgan explained how the machine actually worked.

Chromosomes and Genes

Thomas Morgan built upon the work of Mendel and Miescher through his fruit fly experiments. Using Mendel's laws of segregation and dominance, Morgan developed an explanation for the transmission of parental traits via genes.

As evidenced in Miescher's experiments, DNA, a large biological molecule, can be found in all living cells. In many cells, DNA is coiled tightly into structures called chromosomes. Chromosomes enable each cell in an organism to contain the

James Watson (*left*) and Francis Crick (*right*), the two scientists credited with the discovery of the structure of DNA. James Watson is the second person to make his genome available online.

entire genetic blueprint. Human body cells, for instance, contain forty-six chromosomes each. Chromosomes are divided into sections called genes. Specific genes contain instructions for traits. Morgan determined that many genes make up chromosomes like lightbulbs on a string. One of Morgan's students, Alfred Sturtevant, went on to create the first genetic map in which he placed genes in their proper places on a chromosome.

BARBARA McCLINTOCK

Genes may not be active in every generation. Genes can be activated based on a range of biological factors. Although all organisms contain a genetic code, different combinations of genes result in different organisms. Barbara McClintock, one of the first women elected to the National Academy of Sciences, first proposed this in the late 1940s. McClintock, a plant researcher, observed genetic elements in her plants that seemed to be controlled by other factors. She theorized that while organisms receive a complete set of genetic instructions, certain factors determine which genes are active or inactive.

The DOUBLE HELIX

Without these scientific contributions, scientists would not be able to identify DNA, understand how traits are passed from generation to generation, or recognize the placement of genes on chromosomes. The exact structure of DNA, however, was still unknown.

Francis Crick grew up reading science books and conducting experiments in his kitchen. He studied physics in college and went on to pursue a graduate degree, but World War II interrupted his academic ambitions. During the war, Crick worked on designing mines for the British military. Afterward, Crick decided not to dedicate his career to making weapons. He worked at several biological labs and, while visiting Cambridge University, met a young scientist named James Watson.

James Watson also displayed a passion for science at a young age. While pursuing a graduate degree for ornithology, the study of birds, he read a book on cells. Fascinated by DNA, Watson set out to discover its structure. He and Crick joined forces, working in a lab at Cambridge University. Together, in 1953, based on their theoretical model, they built the first model of DNA using paper cutouts and metal scraps. This incredible discovery led the pair to receive a joint Nobel Prize in 1963.

ROSALIND FRANKLIN

Although James Watson and Francis Crick modeled the structure of DNA, their work would not be possible without experimentation by Rosalind Franklin. Franklin was an

Rosalind Franklin paved the way for Watson and Crick's discovery. She would go on to do foundational work on the structure of the infectious poliovirus.

ambitious and bright student who particularly excelled in science. She earned her doctorate in physical chemistry from Cambridge University in 1945. Being a woman in academia during this time was difficult; university spaces were often segregated by gender. Women were underrepresented in science and mathematics. Franklin was assigned to work on a DNA research project with another scientist. However, her role was misunderstood, and her work was credited to her colleagues. She studied X-ray diffraction, a process used to develop structural pictures of molecules.

While collecting diffraction photos of DNA, Franklin encountered a problem: wet and dry DNA samples produced different X-ray results. She spent a year investigating the problem. She concluded that while the X-rays appeared different, they showed different perspectives of the same chemical structure. DNA was a double-stranded molecule. While she never worked with Watson and Crick, it was Franklin's X-ray work that led to their theoretical model.

DNA STRUCTURE

When Watson and Crick created their model of DNA, it resembled a twisted ladder. Molecules created a pair of parallel sides, and other molecules formed the center rungs. They called this double-stranded structure a **double helix** in a paper published in the journal *Nature* in 1953.

Smaller building blocks, called **nucleotides**, comprise DNA. Each nucleotide has three parts: a 5' carbon sugar, a phosphate, and nitrogen-containing bases. There are two types of **nitrogenous bases**: purines and pyrimidines. The purines in DNA are adenine (A) and guanine (G). The pyrimidines are thymine (T) and cytosine (C). A single base connects to a phosphate-sugar structure. A nitrogenous base, phosphate, and a sugar unit make up a nucleotide. Two chains of nucleotides

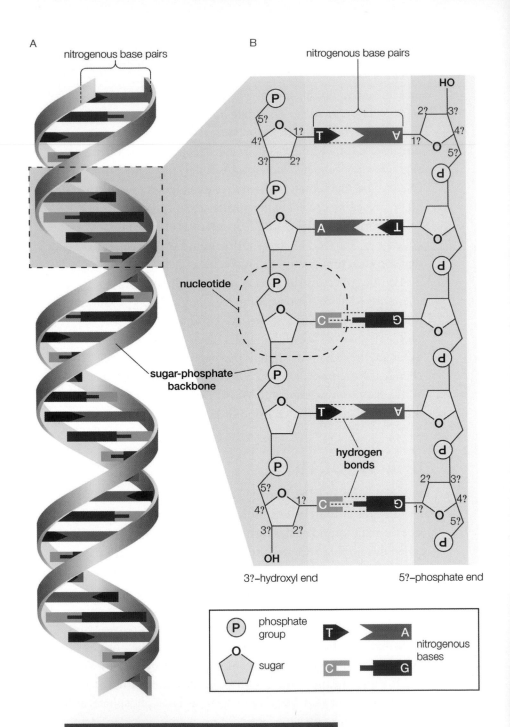

A
nitrogenous base pairs

B
nitrogenous base pairs

P
5?
O
4?   1?
3?   2?

T ▶   ▶ A

HO
2?   3?
1?   O   4?
5?

P

A   ◀ T

d

nucleotide
P
O

C ▭┄┄■ G

d

sugar-phosphate
backbone
P

T ▶   ▷ A

O

hydrogen
bonds

d

P
5?
O
4?   1?
3?   2?
OH

C ▭┄┄■ G

2?   3?
1?   O   4?
5?

d

3?–hydroxyl end

5?–phosphate end

P   phosphate
    group

T ▶   ▶ A
                nitrogenous
                bases
C ▭   ■ G

sugar

Before DNA's function was understood,
it was widely believed that proteins
stored genetic information.

form the double helix, and weak hydrogen bonds connect nitrogenous base pairs.

The base pairs act as an alphabet that forms the instructions of the genetic code. This code provides instructions for carrying out all cellular functions.

Previous research by Edwin Chargaff in 1949 indicated that the bases adenine and thymine appeared in almost equal amounts within an entire set of DNA. Guanine and cytosine were also present in equal numbers. Although Chargaff could not explain it at the time, his research formed the basis for base pairing rules.

As with a written language, the bases are ordered according to certain rules. Pyrimidines and purines are complementary molecules, thus adenine and thymine are always paired while guanine and cytosine always form pairs. Together, these base pairs form the rungs of DNA's ladder. The phosphate and 5' sugar form the sides. Genes are sections of nitrogenous base codes. The particular order of bases within a gene determines the trait.

DNA is copied to ensure that every new cell in an organism has a complete set of genetic code. Because certain cells, such as skin or heart cells, perform specialized jobs, they may not use the entire set of instructions. Instead, certain genes may be utilized for one type of cell and not for another.

The CENTRAL DOGMA

DNA is a double helix, made of nucleotides, and found in every cell in a living organism. It provides instructions for cells to carry out all of life's processes. After James Watson and Francis Crick initially discovered the three-dimensional structure of DNA, questions remained on how exactly cells read DNA code. In 1956, Crick proposed a theory called the central dogma. He argued that a similar, yet unique, molecule called RNA, **ribonucleic acid**, interprets the DNA code. RNA translates the code into **proteins**.

Proteins are biological molecules that perform a wide variety of functions within an organism's body. They contain smaller units called amino acids. Like a train's cars, long chains of amino acids make up a single protein. The four main categories of proteins are structural, defensive, transport, and catalysts. Structural proteins provide support for skeletal structures. Collagen, for example, is a type of structural protein found in tendons. Defensive proteins play a significant role in the immune system. They fight foreign molecules that enter the body. Transport proteins assist cells in acquiring necessary substances and ejecting waste. Lastly, catalysts make chemical reactions within living organisms occur quickly and efficiently. Saliva contains many catalytic proteins that aid in breaking down food particles. Proteins are vital to functioning. They compose about 20 percent of the human body. RNA reads the nitrogenous base pairs and builds proteins in a two-step process: transcription and translation. This process is the fundamental principle of the theory that Francis Crick proposed—an explanation and order of the DNA message codes for proteins.

PROTEIN SYNTHESIS

Dr. Marshall Nirenberg did not begin his academic career studying molecular biology. However, when he decided to focus on DNA, an international scientific race to map the process of protein synthesis was underway. Armed with the knowledge of DNA's chemical structure, base pairing, and the central dogma theory, Nirenberg set out to discover how RNA translated DNA code into proteins. There were two main questions. How many nitrogenous base pairs coded for amino acids? How did the bases correspond to the twenty possible amino acids?

To investigate these issues, Nirenberg developed experiments in which he created a synthetic strand of RNA. He wanted to know the particular amino acid sequence in a protein created by different base pair combinations. RNA follows similar base pairing rules. It uses the nitrogenous bases adenine, guanine, and cytosine. However, it uses uracil instead of thymine. Uracil requires less energy than thymine to produce. Because RNA is created and used at faster rates than DNA, uracil is easier to use.

After many attempts, he finally had a breakthrough. A strand of synthetic RNA with a particular type of nitrogen base was added to twenty different test tubes. Each tube corresponded to one of the twenty possible amino acids. The particular nitrogen base combination of the synthetic RNA caused a chemical response from one particular amino acid.

To break the rest of the code, Nirenberg enlisted the help of his National Institutes of Health colleagues. By 1965, the team became the first to match all twenty amino acids with their corresponding nitrogenous base sequences. They learned that RNA read nitrogenous bases in sets of three called codons. One codon can code for more than one amino acid. RNA carries the DNA code to a protein production site. There, specialized types of RNA translate the code and assemble proteins based on nitrogenous base pair combinations. These experiments helped scientists understand that if there were a mistake in the DNA code, it could result in an incorrect protein. Incorrect proteins could potentially affect the functioning of cells. In addition to these discoveries, subsequent experiments led scientists to understand that the central dogma and the production of proteins, called protein synthesis, were universal. Humans, jellyfish, and trees operate with the same genetic alphabet even if the code creates different messages.

SEQUENCING DNA

The order of amino acids is critical for the creation and function of proteins. Frederick Sanger set out to find a method to identify the order of amino acids in multiple regions of DNA in the mid-1970s. He was the first scientist to successfully sequence a strand of amino acids. Because DNA determines the code for the amino acid order, his success enabled him to sequence DNA nucleotides. This research meant that scientists could determine the order of the four nitrogenous bases in a particular gene or a section of DNA. Knowing the sequence of nucleotides is extremely important. This is what differentiates species. While all living things contain DNA and nitrogenous bases, the order of those bases and the proteins produced may vary widely. The sequence of DNA determines life's diversity.

The task of sequencing DNA, however, would be no simple task. About three billion nitrogenous base pairs make up the forty-six chromosomes in a single human cell. Furthermore, humans have between twenty-five thousand and thirty thousand genes. Determining the entire sequence would be an enormous undertaking for any scientific laboratory.

The ATOM BOMB

Mendel, Morgan, Miescher, Watson, Crick, Franklin, Nirenberg, and Sanger all made vital contributions to the field of genetics. With their work, scientists understand how traits are passed down from one generation to the next. Scientists also know that genes determine specific traits. They know the structure of DNA and the composition of genes and chromosomes. They know that the genetic code contains instructions for proteins, the building blocks of living organisms, and that RNA translates DNA information into proteins.

In 1939, German scientists discovered how to split a uranium atom. The atom is the smallest unit of chemical elements. Uranium, then, is comprised of uranium atoms. Within these smaller units, a large amount of energy is stored. When an atom splits, stored energy is released. This process is called fission. This energy is so strong the German scientists saw the potential to harness this power in a weapon with explosive properties.

With the world at war, a weapon with this potential destructiveness could devastate an opponent's country. With the news of the Germans' research, the United States, a member of the Allied forces, funded a project to design and build an atomic bomb before the Axis powers did. The secret project was named the Manhattan Project. The United States dropped two of the bombs produced by the Manhattan Project on the Japanese cities of Hiroshima and Nagasaki.

The government conducted many tests before the bombing of Japan. Radiation is a side effect of atomic weapons. Radiation has devastating effects on the human body, down to the molecular level. It causes long-term damage to cells and the DNA contained within them. Because children inherit the DNA of their parents, these effects can be passed down through generations. Radiation damages DNA through the process of **mutation**. A DNA mutation simply means a change in one or more nitrogenous bases. Because the bases are the instructions for proteins, mutations can lead to drastic changes in traits.

However, it is important to remember that DNA mutations are neutral. They can have positive, negative, or neutral effects on an organism. An example of positive mutation would be a person that is immune to the human immunodeficiency virus, or HIV. A mistake in the DNA causes the production of an incorrect protein. The virus cannot bind to the irregularly shaped receptor protein.

Changes in DNA can, however, sometimes result in adverse effects. Certain genetic diseases and cancer are examples of negative genetic mutations. Sickle cell disease, for instance, is the result of a mutation that causes red blood cells to be abnormally shaped. These cells cannot move efficiently through the bloodstream, causing many painful, lifelong symptoms. It is also possible for changes in DNA to result in no discernable change in proteins or traits.

Because atomic weapon testing indicated the potential of radiation, it became a major concern to the United States government. After the deployment of the atomic bomb, Congress ordered the Atomic Energy Commission along with the Energy Research and Development Administration to study the possible damage of radiation on DNA. This research was necessary to begin developing treatments for potential negative DNA mutations.

A complete map of human DNA would enable researchers to understand the effects of atomic radiation. The government's commission would lead to an enormous research project, the analysis of more than twenty-five thousand genes, which would span ten years. This project would sequence, map, and record the entire human genetic code.

Linus Pauling and the Triple Helix

While James Watson and Francis Crick were theorizing about the structure of DNA and Rosalind Franklin was performing her X-ray experiments, another scientist was investigating the mystery of DNA structure.

Linus Pauling is considered one of the greatest scientists of the twentieth century. He primarily studied chemistry and biochemistry along with being a well-known peace activist. While his interests were varied, Pauling spent time researching the structure of DNA. He proposed a triple helix model. This structure, however, contained a major flaw.

Pauling argued that the nitrogenous bases faced outward while the phosphate-sugar structures faced inward. This model, however, is chemically impossible. The phosphates that are part of a DNA nucleotide are negatively charged and repel one another. If the center of DNA were made up of these phosphates, the negatively charged molecules would repel one another and rip the structure apart. Despite the inaccuracy of his proposal, Pauling went on to have many great accomplishments. In fact, he is the only person to have individually received two unrelated Nobel Prizes: a Nobel Prize in Chemistry in 1954 and the Nobel Peace Prize in 1962.

Biston betularia specimens, or peppered moths, live in temperate climates and are nocturnal. During the day, the moths spend a great deal of time hiding from their primary predators, birds.

CHAPTER 2

The Science of the Genetic Code

As discussed in chapter 1, DNA, deoxyribonucleic acid, is the genetic blueprint for all living things. Each cell in a living organism contains DNA, the instructions for protein creation.

Eukaryotic cells make up multicellular organisms, such as plants and animals. These cells contain complex substructures called organelles that perform specific functions much like organs in the body. One of these structures, the nucleus, holds the DNA and directs the functioning of the cell.

DNA is a type of biological molecule known as a nucleic acid. Smaller units called nucleotides make up nucleic acids. A phosphate, sugar, and nitrogenous base form a single nucleotide. Nucleic acids are classified based on the type of sugar utilized in the nucleotide. DNA is a double-stranded molecule; phosphates and deoxyribose sugar make up the sides, and weak hydrogen bonds connect the nitrogenous bases. The pyrimidine, cytosine, and thymine pair with the purines guanine and adenine to form the rungs of the double helix.

RNA, ribonucleic acid, is a single stranded nucleic acid. Its nucleotides contain phosphate, ribose sugar instead of deoxyribose, and a single row of nitrogenous bases. RNA also uses guanine, adenine, and cytosine. However, due to the short life of RNA, it uses the pyrimidine uracil instead of thymine, as uracil is faster to produce. There are multiple forms of RNA, and they play various roles in cellular processes.

DNA REPLICATION and MITOSIS

Humans grow and develop in observable ways: newborns grow into toddlers, children develop into teenagers, and teenagers mature into adults. The cause of this maturation process occurs at the cellular level. Groups of cells form tissues, and groups of tissues compose organs. When new cells are produced, new tissue is made and body structures grow. For instance, specialized cells called neurons form brain tissue. Different regions of the human brain contain groups of brain tissue. Many new brain cells are formed in the early years of human life. The swift growth of neurons results in the rapid increase in brain volume in children.

The human body contains many different types of cells, and each has a unique function. Cells perform their assigned duties until they divide into new cells to ensure that organisms mature and life processes continue properly. Human skin acts as the largest barrier against disease and other potentially harmful invaders. The average human body has billions of skin cells, and between thirty thousand and forty thousand are shed per hour. Because of this rapid removal, a new supply must constantly be available. Skin cells divide rapidly to produce new cells and maintain the body's defense system.

Before cell division, cells must undergo DNA **replication**. During this process, a copy of the entire genetic code is produced. Replication ensures that the two new cells produced during cell division, known as daughter cells, have an identical copy of the DNA.

DNA replication occurs in the nucleus. It is a semiconservative process; each DNA strand serves as a template for the new strand. Half of the resulting double helix is from the original strand, and the other half is a new, complementary strand.

DNA resembles a ladder, and it must be separated before replication. DNA helicase, a special type of protein called an enzyme, unzips the ladder into two complementary pieces by breaking the hydrogen bonds that connect the nitrogenous base pairs. Using each side as a template, another enzyme, DNA polymerase, adds matching nitrogenous bases to each side. At the end of the process, two new, complete DNA molecules are formed from the original strand, each made up of one old strand and one new strand. New cells will then have a complete set of identical genetic material.

The Cell Cycle

Body cells, such as heart, skin, and brain cells, develop and divide through a process called the **cell cycle**. The cell cycle has three major stages: interphase, **mitosis**, and cytokinesis. Interphase is the longest period of a cell's life. During this phase, cells grow, replicate their DNA, take in nutrients, and remove wastes. While in interphase, cells also undergo certain checkpoints to gauge when cell replication should occur and if the cell is healthy enough to begin the process. Many cells will divide when they reach a certain size. Like boats, a cell can only be a certain size and volume to function properly. The larger a cell becomes, the more difficulty it has in transporting materials in and out. When a cell reaches its size limit, it undergoes a final check before proceeding into cell division.

Mitosis is a complex process involving several sub-stages. The first, prophase, involves the condensing of the **chromosomes**. The DNA coils into chromosomes, tightly wound structures, like yarn wrapped into a ball. While the DNA within each cell could reach the moon and back multiple times, it is coiled into forty-six individual chromosomes. The number of chromosomes varies in different organisms dependent on the amount of genetic material. The fruit flies studied by Thomas Morgan, for instance, have only eight chromosomes.

In the second subphase, metaphase, the chromosomes line up in the center of the cell. The centromere, a chromosome's centerpiece, connects to strands called spindle fibers. Chromosomes have two short arms and two arms joined by the centromere. They resemble the letter X. During the third sub-stage of mitosis, anaphase, each X-shaped chromosome is split in half and pulled apart toward opposite ends of the cell. Telophase, the final sub-stage, involves the chromosomes dispersing back into free-form DNA.

Cells contain a gel-like substance called cytoplasm. During the final stage of the cell cycle, the cytoplasm pinches in the center and breaks into two daughter cells. Cytokinesis, the last phase of the cell cycle, results in two new daughter cells. Each new body cell contains identical copies of the entire genetic code.

MEIOSIS

Gregor Mendel discovered that organisms inherit a version of every trait from both parents. The entire genetic code to its offspring is passed on in gametes or sex cells. Organisms produce gametes and when combined through a process called fertilization form new life. Although the process of gamete division is similar to the way body cells divide, there are additional steps to ensure that each gamete contains a unique set of genes.

Every body cell in an organism contains two copies of every chromosome. This is called the diploid chromosome number. Fruit flies, for instance, have a diploid number of 8. Because different plants and animals have different numbers of chromosomes, the diploid number of any organism can be written as 2N.

Gametes, on the other hand, contain only half the number of chromosomes, as fertilization combines the genetic material of two unique organisms. The number of chromosomes found in a gamete is called the haploid number. For example, a fruit fly gamete contains only half the diploid number; therefore, the fruit fly's haploid number equals 4, or half of 8. Gametes contain half the number of chromosomes so that when two combine, the resulting first cell of an organism has a complete but unique combination of genetic material, 50 percent from each parent's gamete.

Meiosis is divided into the same sub-stages as mitosis. The major difference is that the sub-stages prophase, metaphase, anaphase, and telophase occur twice. While mitosis involves one cell becoming two daughter cells, a single gamete will divide twice to become four new cells. The daughter cells each contain a unique combination of DNA. This is why all siblings of the same parents have different characteristics. They each have a specific combination of their parents genes, randomly combined to form a brand-new human. Identical twins are an exception and have the exact same genetic blueprint, resulting in identical **phenotypes**.

MENDELIAN GENETICS

Mendel's experiments did not only yield rules for the inheritance of traits. He also demonstrated that organisms inherit two forms of a gene, called **alleles**. For each gene, an organism receives an allele from each parent. It may be two of the same alleles or two different alleles. Mendel also showed that it is possible to predict which of the two alleles will be expressed in the offspring.

A **Punnett square** is a tool used to predict the probability of possible outcomes from a particular parental cross. Recall that in pea plants, yellow seed color is a dominant trait and green seeds are recessive. Whenever an organism inherits

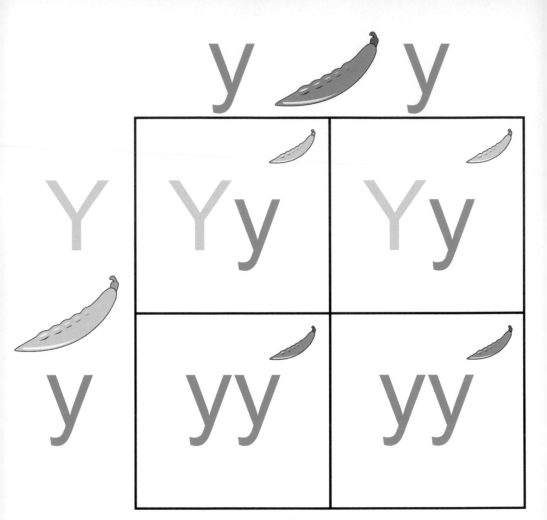

Punnett squares predict all possible combinations of parents' genes. Reginald Punnett developed this genetic tool by studying the feather colors of chickens.

a dominant trait, it will be present in the offspring. Because organisms inherit two variations of a trait from their parents, there are several possible combinations. **Homozygous** refers to two of the same alleles, either two dominant or two recessive. In Mendel's pea plants, two yellow seed alleles would be considered homozygous dominant. The pair of genes inherited for a trait is called the **genotype**. A homozygous dominant genotype, in this example, would result in yellow seeds. Phenotype refers to the physical outcome. If a pea plant inherited the gene for the recessive trait from both parents, green seeds, this homozygous recessive genotype would result in a green seed phenotype.

An organism can also inherit two different alleles, a dominant and a recessive, for a trait. This genotype is called **heterozygous**. If a pea plant were heterozygous for seed color, it would inherit one yellow seed allele and one green seed allele. This heterozygous genotype will result in the expression of the dominant phenotype. Therefore, the pea plant would have yellow seeds.

Punnett squares are simple tools used to predict the likelihood of genotypes and phenotypes based on the parents' genotype. A monohybrid cross compares two parental genotypes to predict the inheritance of one trait.

Using a Punnett square, parental genotypes are written on the sides of a square divided into four boxes. Each box is filled with an allele from the parents' genotype. Scientists can then predict the likelihood of each possibility—homozygous dominant, homozygous recessive, or heterozygous—out of four possibilities. Dominant alleles are represented by a capital letter and recessive by a lowercase letter. If two plants that are heterozygous for seed color (Yy) mate, there is a 25 percent chance their offspring will be homozygous dominant with yellow seeds (YY), a 25 percent chance of homozygous recessive for green seeds (yy), and a 50 percent chance of a heterozygous genotype and a yellow seed phenotype.

ALTERNATIVE MODES of INHERITANCE

Some traits in humans, such as dimples or freckles, follow Mendel's rules of inheritance. A baby will have freckles if he or she inherits at least one dominant allele for the trait. Other traits, however, are inherited in more complex ways.

For example, there are four possible blood types in humans. While a person can inherit only two alleles, there are more than two possibilities, or **multiple alleles**, for blood type within the human population. Humans can inherit the A-type allele or the B-type allele that result in A type blood or B type blood respectively. Humans can also have an allele for neither A or B, which results in the recessive O-type blood. However, both the A and B alleles are dominant to the O allele; a combination of A and B alleles results in the blood type AB. These two alleles are codominant. When inherited alleles are codominant, both phenotypes are expressed. A black and white cat, for example, inherited alleles for both white and black fur. Neither completely dominates and so both are apparent in the cat.

Multiple dominant alleles can also result in a mixed phenotype. This type of inheritance, **incomplete dominance**, results in a blend of two dominant alleles. Red and white petal color in roses, for example, are both dominant. When a rose inherits a dominant red allele from one parent flower and the allele for white petal color from another, the rose will have a blend of the two dominant alleles, resulting in pink petals.

Traits inherited via the **sex chromosomes** are the final example of non-Mendelian forms of inheritance. Humans have twenty-three pairs of chromosomes. Twenty-two of the chromosome pairs are called **autosomes** and are present in both males and females. The twenty-third pair, the sex chromosomes, come in two forms, the X chromosome and Y chromosome, characterized by their shape. These chromosomes determine the sex of the organism. Females have two X chromosomes, XX. The combination XY results in a male. Particular traits are inherited based on genes located on the X chromosome. Because men have only one X chromosome, when they inherit a recessive allele, it results in the recessive phenotype. For instance, red-green color blindness is a result of sex-linked inheritance. Because the recessive allele is carried on the X chromosome, men are more

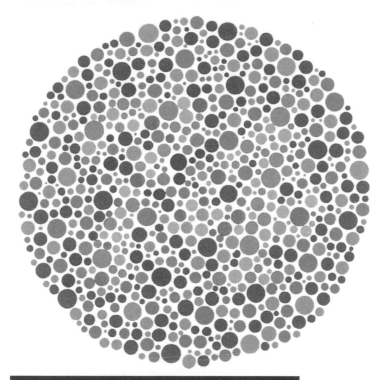

The most common form of color blindness, red-green, can be detected using a simple test like the one pictured here. Identifying the number indicates the ability to discern the two separate colors.

likely to be color blind. Women, on the other hand, have two X chromosomes and are less likely to inherit two recessive alleles that result in color blindness.

MUTATIONS

DNA's code is so extensive that if it were to be stretched out, it would reach to the moon and back multiple times. The process of DNA replication copies the entire set of nucleic acid bases. Sometimes during the copying process, mistakes are made. Imagine copying a book over and over. Here and there a letter might be missed or copied incorrectly. Similarly, errors copying the nitrogenous bases can occur during

DNA replication. A change in DNA, a mutation, can alter the phenotype of an organism. The word "mutation" has a negative connotation in popular culture; however, mutations are neutral. Blue eyes, for instance, are a mutation that occurred in the human population between six thousand and ten thousand years ago. A mistake took place during DNA replication in one human, and this altered DNA code was passed down through multiple generations.

Mutations can be a driving force in a species' survival. In pre–Industrial Revolution England, the peppered moth was primarily white with dark spots to blend in with trees in the area. These moths were camouflaged, making it difficult for predators, such as birds, to locate them from above. However, during the early 1800s, more and more factories were constructed, and they released large amounts of dark pollution into the air. This soot began to stain the peppered moths' light-colored habitat. While the majority of the moth population was also lightly colored to blend in with the environment, a small subset was darker due to a genetic mutation that caused a change in pigmentation. As the trees became heavily covered in soot, predators could spot the light-colored moths quickly. The darker moths survived and passed on the trait for their particular color. In a short amount of time, the majority of the moth population sported the darker pigmentation. The color mutation, then, was beneficial for the darker moths and allowed them to survive and reproduce.

While particular mutations can be helpful, they can also cause biological problems and disorders. Just as there can be different types of mistakes made when writing or copying text, there are several types of DNA mutations.

Point Mutations

A change in a single nucleotide is called a point mutation. One type of point mutation is a substitution in which one base is exchanged for another. If the template strand, for example, has

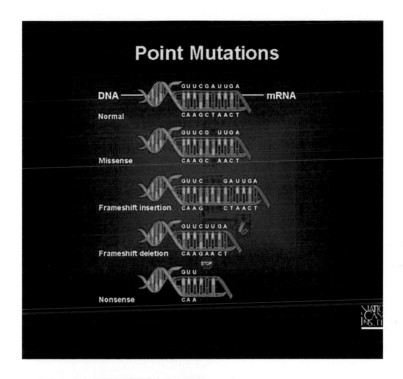

Point Mutations

DNA → ← mRNA

Normal

Missense

Frameshift insertion

Frameshift deletion

Nonsense

Genetic mutations are extremely common; in fact, each of us carries an average of sixty mutations from our parents.

a guanine (G), the DNA helicase should add a cytosine (C) to the complementary strand according to the base pairing rules. If an adenine (A) were paired with it instead, this would be an example of a substitution. Point mutations usually do not have a detrimental effect on the organism as nucleotides are read in groups of three during protein synthesis, so a single change results in a single amino acid change. For example, if a single letter is changed in the sentence THE FAT CAT ATE THE RAT so that it reads THE FAT BAT ATE THE RAT, it changes the meaning of one word rather than the entire sentence.

Frameshift Mutations

Insertions and deletions are more severe forms of mutations because they can cause a change to a significantly larger portion of the entire genetic code. An extraneous nitrogenous base results in an insertion. In the example sentence, if an extra T is inserted, it changes the entire meaning of the phrase, resulting in THE FTA TCA TAT ETH ERA T. When an insertion mutation occurs, it changes the order of all codons afterward.

The second type of frameshift mutation, deletions, removes a nitrogen base from the sequence. If the T in "fat" were removed, the sample sentence would read THE FAC ATA TET HER AT. Again, the entire genetic code is altered after the deletion. The alteration of codons changes the amino acids and, thus, changes the proteins produced.

GENETIC DISORDERS
Chromosomal Abnormalities

While neither good nor bad, in some instances, mutations can cause genetic disorders. A genetic disorder is an inherited, lifelong condition that is the result of either a structural or numerical abnormality in the autosomes or a mutation that involves the sex chromosomes. All humans have twenty-two autosomes and one pair of sex chromosomes. Because genetic disorders are the result of mistakes in the genetic code, they are present from birth and noncontagious. They are rare and vary based on which chromosome is affected.

Recall that during meiosis the chromosomes are separated to ensure that each new cell has a single copy of each chromosome. When male and female gametes combine, each new cell has a complete set of genetic material. Numerical chromosomal mutations occur when the chromosomes fail to separate properly. This is called nondisjunction. Nondisjunction can result in a new cell with too many or too

Down Syndrome - Trisomy 21

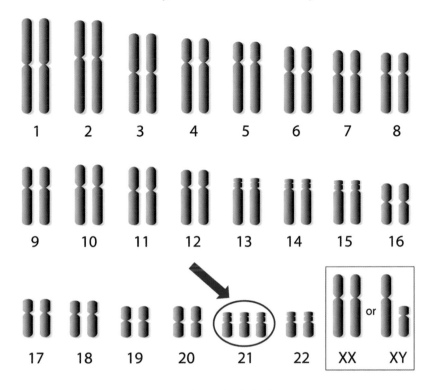

Down syndrome is the most common form of trisomy, caused by an extra copy of chromosome 21.

few of a particular chromosome pair. When a daughter cell has three versions of a chromosome, this is called trisomy.

The most common trisomy, Down syndrome, is the result of an extra chromosome number 21, or trisomy 21. Down syndrome is marked by developmental and intellectual delays and is present in about one out of eight hundred births per year. Disorders caused by trisomy of other chromosomes, such as trisomy 18 and trisomy 13, are less frequent but affect about one in ten thousand and one in sixteen thousand births respectively.

Structural abnormalities result when chromosomes are present but have extra or missing sections. Chromosomes are made up of many sections of genes and resemble an X. They are said to have a "long" arm, the lower parts of the X shape, and "short" arms that make up the upper portion. A missing section, even very small, can cause significant problems. Cri-Du-Chat syndrome, for instance, is the result of the loss of a small portion of chromosome 5's small arm. This disorder is marked by intellectual disabilities, low birth weight, and poor muscle tone. The duplication of chromosomal material can also have harmful effects. Pallister Killian disorder, for instance, is the result of extra information on chromosome 12, also marked by multiple health problems.

Sex chromosomes can also be affected by structural or numerical abnormalities. Klinefelter syndrome, for instance, affects male development as a result of an extra X chromosome to the male genotype of XY. Conversely, Turner syndrome is a chromosomal disorder that affects females. Instead of the female genotype XX, individuals with Turner syndrome have only one X. The second sex chromosome is either missing or structurally altered.

Mendelian Inheritance

Some genetic disorders are inherited following Mendel's pattern of single gene inheritance and the rules of dominance and are typically categorized as autosomal dominant, autosomal recessive, and sex-linked.

Autosomal dominant disorders are inherited through genes on the autosomal chromosomes 1 through 22. These disorders can be passed on from either parent. The mutated gene is dominant; if it is present in the genotype, the person will have the disorder. Individuals can inherit the mutated trait from just one parent and pass it on to their offspring. Either a heterozygous genotype or a homozygous genotype will result in the disorder and may be passed on.

Huntington disorder is an autosomal dominant disorder that affects long-term brain functioning. A mutated gene causes misshapen proteins to alter the ability of brain cells, or neurons, to function. Over time, this deterioration can lead to involuntary muscle movement and lowered mental functioning. Marfan syndrome, another autosomal disorder, is the result of a mutation that affects the production of a stabilizing material for muscle tissue. Individuals with Marfan syndrome may experience heart and vision problems. They also have elongated arms and fingers as a result of unstable muscle structures. Scientists believe that the sixteenth president of the United States, Abraham Lincoln, may have had this genetic disorder.

Other disorders are inherited in an autosomal recessive pattern. These disorders manifest only as the result of a homozygous recessive genotype. Individuals with autosomal recessive disorders must inherit an allele for the disorder from both parents.

Cystic fibrosis is an autosomal recessive disorder that causes the body to produce excess mucus. It can cause respiratory and digestive problems and prohibits healthy organ functioning.

Sickle cell disease is a result of a point mutation in which a thymine (T) substitutes for adenine (A). If a child inherits the recessive allele from both parents, he or she will inherit this autosomal recessive disorder. It is also possible to inherit a recessive allele from one parent and a dominant, normal allele from the other. Individuals with the heterozygous genotype are not affected; instead, they are said to be sickle cell trait carriers. While they are not symptomatic, carriers can still pass on the recessive allele. Individuals with sickle cell disease can experience stroke, pain, or even death.

Hemophilia is an example of a disorder inherited through the sex chromosomes. Because of a mutation in a gene responsible for producing a blood-clotting agent, individuals with hemophilia can experience excessive bleeding even after minor procedures and injuries. The genes associated with hemophilia are located on the X chromosome. The disorder is more common in males as they have one X chromosome. If a male inherits the mutated gene, he will have the disorder.

A GENETIC MAP

The genetic code of all organisms is complex and self-replicating. Changes in DNA can result in favorable changes that enable a species' survival. Mutations can also result in harmful changes, causing disorders that can significantly inhibit survival or even be fatal. A map of a species' entire genetic code, or **genome**, would help scientists and doctors understand how genes interact to create diversity and life.

By the mid-twentieth century, the field of genetics had rapidly grown from Gregor Mendel's experiments with pea plants. Scientists understood the structure of DNA, how it codes for proteins, and how DNA replicates itself to ensure that the entire genetic code is passed on. Despite all these advances, discoveries of new genetic disorders, such as Down syndrome, illuminated the need for a complete blueprint of the human genome. A map could help scientists understand the effects of mutations and begin to study ways to treat and possibly prevent them.

Theophilus Painter and Human Chromosomes

While scientists understand that chromosomes and genes were the mechanisms for DNA inheritance in the early twentieth century, a debate remained about exactly how many chromosomes humans had.

In the early 1920s, a scientist named Theophilus Painter set out to discover the exact number of chromosomes within a given human cell. He did this by studying tissue samples from one individual. After examining different sections under a microscope, Painter determined that human cells contain a total of forty-eight chromosomes. However, given the technology at the time, it was difficult to view all the chromosomes at once. Also, because scientists did not understand the nature of chromosomal mutations, there was no way for Painter to know if the individual whose tissue he examined had a normal, representative number of chromosomes.

A scientist named Joe Hin Tjio, along with his partner Albert Levan, expanded Painter's method and examined cells only in a particular sub-stage of mitosis, prophase, because the chromosomes were condensed and easier to see. They also looked at more than one individual's tissue samples to eliminate experimental error. From their experiments, they determined that every human cell contains forty-six individual chromosomes.

Understanding chromosomal number allowed scientists to detect abnormalities. In 1959, Jerome Lejeune and colleagues discovered that Down syndrome, a disorder already known to the medical and scientific community, is caused by a third chromosome 21 and that the excess genetic material affects development.

CHAPTER 3

The Major Players of the Human Genome Project

The scientific community made an astonishing announcement in April 2003. A group of scientists declared that they had successfully identified all 3.2 billion nitrogenous bases in the human genome. Called the Human Genome Project, groups of scientists, labs, and government agencies worked together to complete the project. It took more than a decade and was one of the most important advances of the twenty-first century.

Sequencing all the nitrogenous bases was an ambitious goal. The Human Genome Project required scientists to accomplish several difficult things. First, they needed to physically break apart the entire double helix. Then, they had to map the genes on all forty-six chromosomes. Mapping allowed them to identify all the bases in order. Last, they had to apply their discovery to solve real world problems.

Project completion, however, would not have been possible without the work of many individual scientists. Scientific discoveries build upon the work of previous research. The project was made possible by the discoveries of Gregor Mendel, Thomas Morgan, Francis Crick, and James Watson. Several different prominent leaders ensured the Human Genome Project's success.

GENE LINKAGE

During meiosis, chromosomes separate to create gametes with different genes. Gregor Mendel determined specific rules for how organisms inherit dominant and recessive traits. In 1905, a group of geneticists discovered an exception to Mendel's rules. William Bateson, Edith Rebecca Saunders, and Reginald C. Punnett studied Mendel's species of pea plants. The scientists observed that some traits appeared together and more often than others. The researchers decided that their results meant that certain genes were connected. These traits might be inherited together, or genetically linked, instead of randomly divided into the daughter cells. Reginald Punnett was also responsible for the creation of the Punnett square, the tool used to predict what traits offspring would have.

GENE MAPPING

The work of Punnett, Saunders, and Bateson was then used by Alfred Sturtevant to create the first **gene map**. Sturtevant worked with Thomas Morgan on his fruit fly experiments. He created the first gene map using fruit fly chromosomes. Sturtevant studied three traits: eye, wing, and body characteristics. He estimated how often these traits were inherited together and used the data to create a map of the genes.

Sturtevant's work showed that the farther apart genes were on a chromosome, the more likely they were to be inherited separately. Separate genes will form different combinations within the new cell. The closer genes are, the more likely they hold the instructions for similar traits. The process of gene mapping is similar to a road map. Gene maps show the position, spacing, and any particular markers, like landmarks, of genes on a chromosome.

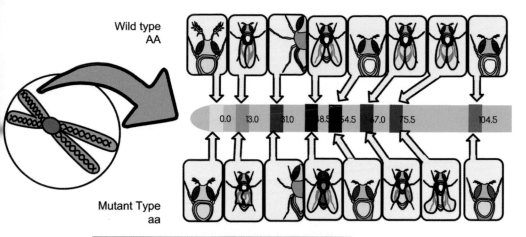

Wild type
AA

| 0.0 | 13.0 | 31.0 | 48.5 | 54.5 | 67.0 | 75.5 | | 104.5 |

Mutant Type
aa

Blood and tissue samples are used to create genetic maps. Maps are available through a variety of sources including the National Institutes of Health and the Genome Browser of the University of California.

The process of gene mapping was important to the success of the Human Genome Project. Dr. Sturtevant received the National Medal of Science in 1968 in honor of his discovery.

RECOMBINANT DNA

In 1973, Herbert Boyer and Stanley Cohen developed a method called recombinant DNA technology. This process combines genetic material from two different animals. All organisms use the same nitrogenous bases in their DNA. However, these bases appear in different amounts and orders. These differences are responsible for all of the diversity of life. Boyer and Cohen's process involved inserting genetic information from one organism into another's DNA. Boyer and Cohen successfully performed their first experiment with bacteria DNA. They were surprised to find the genetic information present in the next generation of bacteria cells. This meant that not only could scientists change genetic material, but that those changes could be passed on.

Boyer and Cohen then performed another experiment. The researchers successfully placed genetic information from a toad into bacteria DNA. They showed that DNA from two completely different animals could be combined. Organisms make different substances based on the instructions in their DNA. Their cells also reproduce at different rates. The reason that recombination was such an exciting new field of research is because scientists could make organisms, like bacteria, produce useful substances quickly. This technology could also help organisms produce substances to help them survive, and this meant that changing DNA could help to cure genetic disorders.

Boyer and Cohen's research also suggested that scientists can arrange and change DNA. However, scientists at the time were concerned about the possible negative use of this new scientific knowledge. They created a set of rules for scientists working with recombinant technology.

Sequencing DNA

Genes can vary in size from around two thousand base pairs to more than twenty thousand. The process of gene mapping first developed by Sturtevant is very useful. Gene maps, however, do not reveal the actual order of the bases. If the order is unknown, scientists cannot understand how a gene works in a particular organism. Gene maps also do not show the effects of mutation on genes.

Gene sequencing, on the other hand, determines the exact order of the nitrogenous bases for a certain gene. The process is similar to putting individual letters in order. The unique arrangement of bases in a gene determines the particular protein needed. Sequencing allows scientists to identify and study specific genes. Understanding the exact order of the

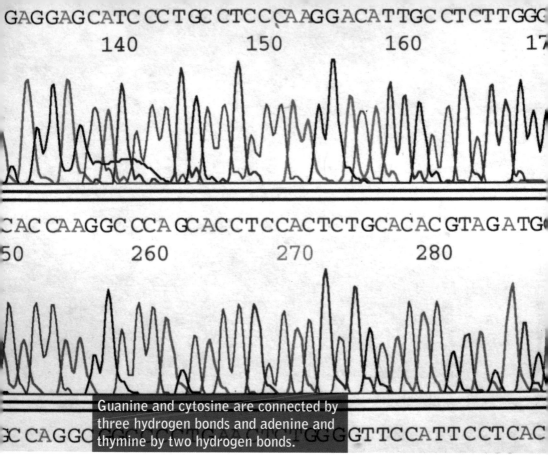

GAG GAG CATC CC T GC CTC C CA GG ACA T TGC CT CT T GGG

140   150   160   17

CAC CA AG GC CCA GC AC CT C CAC TCT GCAC AC GTA G A TG

50   260   270   280

Guanine and cytosine are connected by three hydrogen bonds and adenine and thymine by two hydrogen bonds.

GC CAG GC GCC CGT C AA CT GGG GT TC CATT CCT CAC

bases allows scientists to study changes in DNA and how genes interact.

    Scientists working on the Human Genome Project needed to create a map of all the genes in all forty-six chromosomes. They also needed to determine the order of all of the bases. Frederick Sanger, a Nobel Laureate, created one of the first genome sequencing methods.

    Frederick Sanger was born August 13, 1918. His father, a doctor, encouraged a love for science in his son. Sanger enrolled at the University of Cambridge to study physics and chemistry. However, physics proved very challenging for him. Sanger decided to enroll in a new field of study called biochemistry. Biochemistry is the study of molecules found within living things like DNA and proteins. Sanger excelled in the biological sciences and went on to become a researcher.

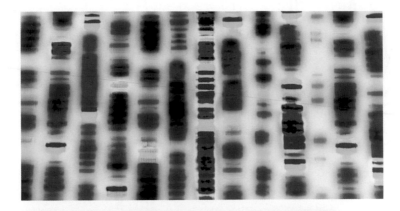

Chromosomes, and the number of genes, do not determine complexity of an organism. Humans have twenty-three pairs and chimpanzees have twenty-four, while fruit flies only have eight.

Sanger studied a special type of protein called insulin. Amino acids make up proteins. The code for each amino acid is found in DNA sequences. Sanger's research involved sequencing all the amino acids that formed insulin. As a result of his research, Sanger was awarded the 1958 Nobel Prize for Chemistry.

Sanger then joined the Medical Research Council in 1962. His work on insulin provided a stepping-stone for his next big research project. Along with other important scientists like Francis Crick, he worked at sequencing the nitrogenous bases in a section of DNA.

Sanger developed one of the most successful methods of gene sequencing. Previous ways of reading the bases took a long time and could only order small number bases. In the Sanger method, DNA is copied using dyed nitrogen bases. Matching base pairs are added to the new strand during DNA replication. When these special bases are added, they cause replication to stop at different points. This results in DNA segments of different lengths. These fragments are then ordered like a puzzle. Researchers can use the order of the dyed bases to read the original sequence.

Frederick Sanger remained at Cambridge during World War II as a conscientious objector because of his Quaker religion.

In 1977, Sanger used his sequencing method to decode the 5,400-base genome of a virus. Then, larger genomes were decoded, like the 172,000-base Epstein-Barr virus. Sanger's new, faster method would be tremendously valuable to the Human Genome Project. Because of his contributions, he was awarded a second Nobel Prize in Chemistry in 1980.

GENETIC MAPPING and SEQUENCING: The GENE FOR HUNTINGTON'S DISEASE

As a researcher at Massachusetts General Hospital in Boston, James Gusella was determined to understand genetic disorders. In 1983, he announced that he and a team of researchers located the gene responsible for Huntington's disease. Research done in Venezuela by Nancy Wexler, a member of the team, contributed to this discovery. She and her team studied the DNA of a large family with the disorder. The identification of the Huntington gene meant that scientists and doctors could begin to investigate new treatments. They could also screen for the DNA mutation in families who wanted to have children.

Dr. Wexler's research methods were based on advances in Sturtevant's genetic mapping. To study potential genetic patterns, DNA is taken from a person's blood cells. If identified, scientists record the strange patterns as markers. These help them find and compare the same section of a gene in other blood samples. While a marker is not one particular gene, it can help researchers identify the location of a gene on a chromosome. Physical genetic mapping, on the other hand, determines the actual location of base sequences on a chromosome. It breaks the DNA into small pieces and then puts them back together. However, physical mapping differs from the Sanger method of sequencing. Maps determine the order of special landmarks on a chromosome like the chapters of a book. A genome sequence, on the other hand, is like the actual sentences of a book.

A PROJECT PROPOSAL
Robert Sinsheimer and Renato Dulbecco

Robert Sinsheimer was an important figure in starting the Human Genome Project. The chancellor of the University of California, Santa Cruz, Sinsheimer had a background in science. He brought his passion for biology into his leadership position. A large amount of money had been donated to Sinsheimer's college to build a high-tech, expensive telescope. UC Santa Cruz did not have enough money to build it, though another university did. Sinsheimer believed that the money should be used for a gene-sequencing project instead. However, the University of California's president denied Sinsheimer's proposal so he organized a conference of leading geneticists. The conference, which took place in Santa Cruz, was to discuss how to fund and start such a complex project. The Santa Cruz conference was successful. While skeptical at first, most of the attendees agreed at the end of the meeting that the project was possible. Planning began right away.

Renato Dulbecco worked at the Salk Institute in 1963 as a cancer researcher. He received the 1975 Nobel Prize in medicine for his research. On March 7, 1986, Dulbecco declared that scientists needed to understand the human genome to progress in treating cancer. He urged scientists to dedicate themselves to this important research.

Charles DeLisi and the Department of Energy

The US government was interested in the effects of atomic bombs after World War II. Atomic bombs cause radiation, and radiation can cause mutations, or changes, to DNA. The US Department of Energy was responsible for making nuclear weapons and exploring nuclear technology. The US Department of Energy helped in the genome project's creation.

Charles DeLisi, the director of the Office of Health and Environment at the Department of Energy, supported genome research. In 1986, DeLisi developed a five-year Department of Energy program to map gene locations and develop technology to enhance sequencing. In 1987, he set aside $4.5 million for the project.

The National Institutes of Health, an organization entirely focused on biological research, was another leader in the project. Leaders of the National Institutes of Health were worried that the Department of Energy would get the majority of government funding. However in 1988, Congress elected to fund both organizations. The National Institutes of Health and the Department of Energy formed a partnership. The Department of Energy focused on technology development, and the National Institutes of Health focused on actual sequencing. James Watson, one of the discoverers of the structure of DNA, was elected to head the National Institutes of Health.

James Watson and the National Institutes of Health

James Watson remained active in the scientific community after he and Francis Crick wrote their paper on the structure of DNA. He became a major leader in the early years of the Human Genome Project. He was elected to lead a section of the National Institutes of Health named the Office of Human Genome Research and eventually renamed the National Center for Human Genome Research.

Watson was an outspoken supporter of the project. He worked on assembling a team of some of the most respected scientists in genetic research. He was also responsible for finding funding for the project in the early years. Watson believed the project would be one of the most important breakthroughs in scientific history. The real potential, Watson argued, would be the project's contribution to the fight against genetic disorders.

> I see an extraordinary potential for human betterment ahead of us. We have at our disposal the ultimate tool for understanding ourselves at the molecular level and for fighting the genetic diseases that diminish the quality of so many of our lives. The time to act is now.

However, despite being a strong leader, Watson did not see the National Institutes of Health's contribution to the project to its completion. Three years after his appointment, in 1992, he resigned from his leadership role as a result of a dispute with the head of the institute. Watson's aggressive support allowed the new program to receive funding. During his time as leader, he assisted in creating an initial five-year research plan for the Human Genome Project.

LEADERS of the HUMAN GENOME PROJECT
Craig Venter

J. Craig Venter was born October 14, 1946, in Salt Lake City, Utah. He and his family moved to San Francisco, California, where he attended high school. Venter enjoyed surfing and carpentry growing up. After high school, Venter enlisted in the US Navy and was trained as a medical corpsman during the Vietnam War. During his service, he was inspired to help fill the knowledge gaps he saw while working at the Da Nang Hospital. After his tour of duty, Venter enrolled as a premedical student at the University of California, San Diego. However, he became fascinated with the science that his premedical classes were based on and decided to focus on research instead. He graduated with his bachelor's degree in biochemistry and a Ph.D. in physiology and pharmacology in six short years.

Venter then accepted a position as a professor at State University in Buffalo, New York. In 1984, he joined the National Institutes of Health as a genetics researcher. During his time at the institute, Venter discovered ESTs, or expressed sequence tags, and developed a method of using ESTs in gene identification. ESTs are short sequences of complementary DNA strands that act as labels that are interpreted by automatic DNA sequencing machines. The EST method does not sequence the entire genome. Instead, it focuses on specific sequences responsible for making proteins. It was, Venter proclaimed, the fastest and cheapest way to sequence the genome. As a researcher for National Institutes of Health, Venter was extremely enthusiastic about the Human Genome Project even though he disagreed with James Watson's five-year

The first DNA sequencing machine was invented by Lloyd Smith in 1987 and utilized the Sanger sequencing method. Modern machines are much faster, but still are very expensive.

plan. Venter also felt that only one organization should work on the project instead of many different research groups.

Venter and James Watson disagreed about the effectiveness of his EST method. Watson believed that the entire genome should be sequenced instead of the EST shortcut. Venter decided to apply for patents, or individual ownership, for the gene sequences discovered through his research. This created a large disagreement in the National Institutes of Health. The patenting controversy contributed to the resignation of James Watson, who opposed patenting genetic material. The Patent Office eventually rejected Venter's application.

In 1992, Venter left the institute and founded his own private research institute, the Institute for Genomic Research (TIGR). In 1995, Venter shocked the scientific community when he announced that he and another TIGR scientist, Hamilton Smith, had successfully sequenced the entire 1,750-base genome of a bacteria. What made this announcement so incredible was the fact that the team produced these results in less than a year.

Venter did this through another new sequencing technique he developed. He called the process "shotgun genome sequencing." Shotgun genome sequencing was different from other previous processes, such as the Sanger method. The Sanger method could only sequence small numbers of nitrogenous bases at a time. While the procedure was somewhat similar to physical gene mapping, Venter's approach produced a complete genome sequence.

Like physical mapping, his method broke the entire genome into many tiny fragments. Then, an advanced machine put all the pieces back together in a short amount of time.

In 1998, eight years after the official start of the Human Genome Project, Venter turned his full attention to human genome sequencing. He left the nonprofit TIGR and founded a for-profit, Celera Genomics. The goal of the new organization was to produce genetic and sequencing technology. His lab developed sequencing machines that were able to rapidly process large amounts of information.

Dr. Venter and the Celera team would eventually be one of the most important contributors to the Human Genome Project. His techniques were essential for the completion of the project in 2003. He and his team were also responsible for the complete sequencing of the rat, mouse, and fruit fly genomes.

Francis Collins

The discoveries and technology invented by Venter and Celera were extremely important to the completion of the Human Genome Project. Francis Collins was another leading scientist in the project's completion. Collins was the director of the National Institutes of Health from 1993 until 2008.

Collins grew up on a farm in the Shenandoah Valley in Virginia and was homeschooled until the sixth grade.

Throughout high school and college, Collins focused on chemistry and math. In an interview, he recalled having little interest in his biology class.

> I also took biology in high school and I didn't like it at all. It was focused on memorization. Learning the parts of the crayfish was a typical assignment. I didn't think that was very interesting. I might have made a bit of a mistake. I didn't appreciate that biology also had principles and logic. I concluded at the age of 15 or 16 that I had no interest in biology, or medicine, or any of those aspects of science that dealt with this messy thing called life. It just wasn't organized, and I wanted to stick with the nice pristine sciences of chemistry and physics, where everything made sense. I wish I had learned a little sooner that biology could be fun as well.

Collins received a degree in chemistry from the University of Virginia in 1970. He then attended Yale University and received a Ph.D. in physical chemistry in 1974. During his studies, Collins took a biochemistry course where he learned about RNA and DNA. Fascinated by these molecules, intrigued by the rapidly growing field of genetics, and filled with a desire to study something more directly beneficial than physics, Collins enrolled as a medical student at the University of North Carolina. He graduated with his medical degree in 1977.

Collins focused his research on searching for genes associated with genetic disorders. As a researcher at Yale, he developed a technique called positional cloning. This method was based on the concept of gene linkage and physical mapping. Sections of linked genes are studied to locate genes related to a genetic disease. Positional cloning is useful for identifying genetic disorders that scientists do not know much about. Using this technique, Collins and a team of researchers discovered the gene responsible for cystic fibrosis in 1989.

In fact, Collins was so successful in identifying previously unknown genes, he earned the nickname "gene-hunter." Potential cloning also contributed to the work of Nusella and Wexler in identifying the Huntington gene.

In 1993, Collins was invited to be the director of the National Institutes of Health after James Watson's departure. As director, he oversaw the division of the institute working on the Human Genome Project until its completion in 2003. Like James Watson, Collins was a huge supporter and advocate of the project. He believed it to be one of the most significant scientific advances of our time.

An Interview with Francis Collins

Interviewer: Dr. Collins, you had a major change of direction early in your career. You started out as a chemist. You had started a family and were getting a Ph.D. when you changed courses and went to medical school. What was that like?

FC: I was kind of in a crisis. Here I was, already had a kid who was a couple of years old, and I was facing the idea of starting over again, and what to do. And I was pretty shaken up about whether research was the right thing for me or not. So I considered many options, and stayed up many nights wondering which was right. And finally decided, even though it had not been a childhood dream at all, that medicine was a really interesting option for me ... I knew I had this urge to try to do something for other human beings, an urge that I hadn't been able to experience quite in the way I wanted to in the physical sciences.

It took a long time, so I'm sympathetic with young people who find themselves surrounded by others who seem to have zeroed in exactly on what they want to do, and yet they're not so sure themselves whether they've found their dream. I encourage people to take their time.

I now think I'm the luckiest guy in science ... I believe that reading our blueprints, cataloguing our own instruction book, will be judged by history as more significant than even splitting the atom or going to the moon. This is an adventure into ourselves.

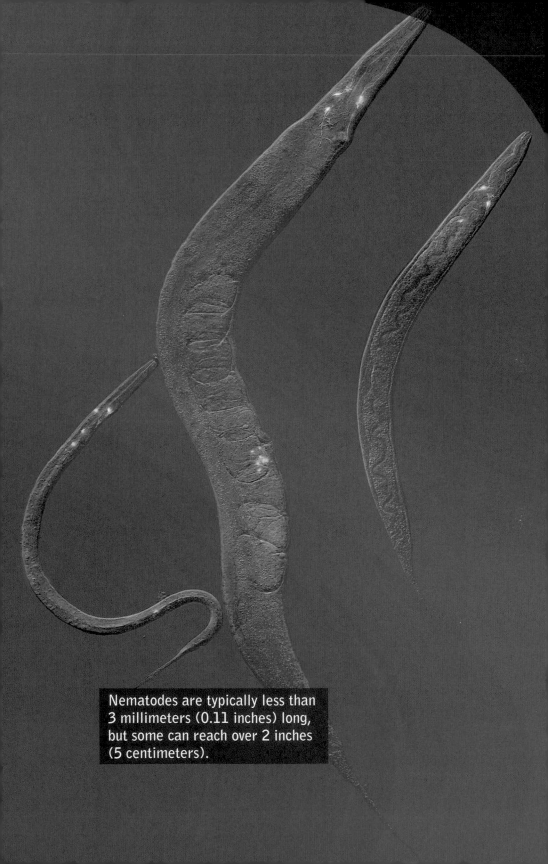

Nematodes are typically less than 3 millimeters (0.11 inches) long, but some can reach over 2 inches (5 centimeters).

CHAPTER 4

The Human Genome

In early 1988, advances in genetic research in the previous decades set the stage for the ambitious Human Genome Project. In October of that year, the National Institutes of Health and Department of Energy signed an agreement to collaborate. Together, they would share objectives, techniques, and data on the sequencing project.

In 1989, the National Institutes of Health established a new office, the National Center for Human Genome Research. Dr. James Watson was appointed leader.

Before the National Institutes of Health and the Department of Energy began their research, they released a five-year plan that outlined the project's goals. They estimated the project would take at least fifteen years and require a yearly $200 million budget.

The Human Genome Project (HGP) had seven long-term goals. The first two goals were to map and sequence the genomes of humans and other organisms. Model organisms would provide examples to researchers working on the more complicated human genome. The third objective was to collect and distribute that data to the public. The National Institutes of Health and the Department of Energy also hoped to address the effects of the project on society. While decoding the human genome had the potential to help scientists understand genetic diseases and develop treatments, the research teams had to consider the possible negative impacts of genetic research.

HGP's remaining goals were to share knowledge among different professions, to develop training for new genetic scientists, and to improve genetic technology.

Each long-term goal was paired with shorter five-year objectives. HGP scientists planned to a have a complete map of all the genes in the human genome with markers, or genetic landmarks, finished by 1998. More landmarks would mean that scientists could easily find genes when conducting research. At the time, scientists believed that the human genome contained more than one hundred thousand genes. As a result of the Human Genome Project's findings, scientists now know there are only about thirty thousand genes total.

Researchers also planned to improve sequencing technology and reduce costs within five years. While the Sanger method was a faster and efficient method, it was still very expensive to sequence large stretches of DNA. Creating software to manage the project, recruiting trainees to work on the project, improving existing technology, and creating partnerships with other industries like the medical field were some other short-term goals.

ETHICAL CONCERNS

While there was considerable excitement in the scientific community at the beginning of the Human Genome Project, there were also many ethical concerns. Researchers must consider how new technology and discoveries may positively and negatively affect people. The Ethical, Legal, and Social Implications program, founded in 1990, was part of the Human Genome Project. The ELSI's purpose was to study and monitor issues raised by human genome sequencing. The purpose of the program was to examine the consequences of genetic research on individuals, families, and society. The ELSI focused on four major concerns. The first was the issue of privacy. Human genome sequencing made it possible to know every detail about someone's genetic blueprint. Scientists worried that genetic differences could lead to unfair treatment. Employers might choose not to hire someone based on his or her genes. Health insurance companies could refuse to give someone insurance. The members of the Human Genome Project knew the importance of genetic research being used in a fair and ethical way.

The ELSI also conducted research on how the medical field could use the Human Genome Project's findings. Doctors and hospitals needed fast and inexpensive ways to perform genetic tests.

How scientists accessed people's genetic information was another area of concern for the ELSI. For many years, scientists were not required to get people's permission, or consent, when doing experiments. For example, scientists could take things, like cells, from individuals without their knowledge or permission. In the case of Henrietta Lacks, for instance, doctors removed some tissue samples from her during a surgical procedure. The cells extracted from Lacks's tissue went on to form the first immortal cell line. The word "immortal" in this case refers to cells that can reproduce indefinitely in a lab. Scientists have used these cells to make many advances in medicine. For instance, experiments conducted with the cell line helped to develop the vaccine for polio. Polio is an infectious disease that quickly spreads from person to person. It affects the nervous system and may eventually result in paralysis. Before the creation of the vaccine, it was most commonly present in children. The immortal cell line contributed to so many scientific advances and launched a multibillion-dollar industry. However, Henrietta Lacks's family did not receive any of the profits. In fact, her children had no idea that their mother's cells were the first to go into space or used to create a life-saving vaccine.

Participants who provided DNA for the Human Genome Project needed to be informed and treated fairly. Telling an experiment participant about the research and receiving permission is called informed consent.

The fourth area handled by the ELSI was educating doctors, politicians, and the public about the effects of genetic research. The public needed to understand all the possible outcomes and results of the project.

Although widely supported, there were also critics of the project. Several prominent scientists argued that it would take away funding and talent from other valuable research. Critics did not believe the proposed timeline was possible. They maintained the project would require even more money than the $3 billion budget. Critics were also concerned with the number of large grants, or money from the government or other agencies, awarded to the project. Opponents worried that the Human Genome Project might take funding away from other important research.

Critics argued that sequencing the entire genome was not the best approach to studying diseases. Instead, they believed that scientists should instead focus on one disease at a time as done in the past.

Conflict also existed within the groups working on the project. In the early years of the project, Dr. Craig Venter promoted his new sequencing method as the best approach. His research focused on finding particular points in DNA for developing new medicine and treatments. Venter believed that sequencing the entire genome was a waste of time. His technique, expressed sequence tags, sequenced only certain sections of DNA. Those sections were blueprints for proteins. Many areas of DNA do not code for proteins referred to as "junk DNA." Venter felt that sequencing junk DNA was not a proper use of funding or time. His opinions, however, conflicted with the goals of Watson and the National Institutes of Health. A debate ensued, ending with the resignation of

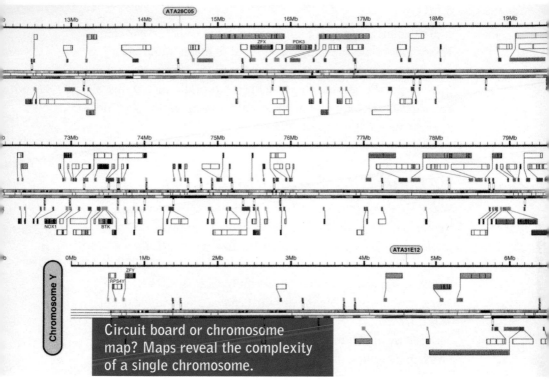

Circuit board or chromosome map? Maps reveal the complexity of a single chromosome.

Watson and the departure of Venter. Francis Collins assumed the leadership role over the institute's genome project division.

A COMPLETE GENETIC MAP

Human Genome Project researchers needed a full map of all forty-six human chromosomes before beginning the sequencing phase of the project. Once scientists had a genetic map, they would be able to order sequenced DNA sections. Eventually, they would have all the genes ordered. The completion of a genetic map would have a positive effect on the medical field. Many identified genes and markers would allow scientists and doctors to quickly discover genes associated with genetic disorders.

A complete map was to be completed by 1995. However, the researchers finished a complete map of all forty-six chromosomes by 1994, a full year ahead of schedule. It also contained more markers than planned for in the five-year plan. The original plan called for six hundred to fifteen hundred markers. The completed map had almost seven thousand. Members of the Human Genome Project proudly shared this accomplishment with the public even as they began to work on the next steps of the project.

HAEMOPHILUS INFLUENZAE

While HGP researchers celebrated their mapping success, Venter and the team at his privately owned company, the Institute for Genomic Research, were making significant progress. In 1995, Venter and another scientist, Dr. Hamilton Smith, announced that they successfully sequenced the entire genome of an organism called *Haemophilus influenzae*. This microscopic organism is a bacteria that causes illness, particularly in children. *H. influenzae* can cause breathing problems, swelling of the brain, and pneumonia.

Venter and his team sequenced the 1,750 genes of *H. influenzae* in less than a year. They did so using Venter's shotgun sequencing method.

The scientific community was amazed at this accomplishment. Venter received a great deal of praise. Supporters believed that this was a breakthrough in genetics and biology.

However, some scientists continued to express doubt about Venter's shotgun sequencing method. They argued that it might not work on an organism with a much larger genome, like a human. Venter was disappointed with this reaction. Ignoring the benefits of a faster sequencing method, he argued, was like ignoring the invention of the automobile.

The research team compared the genes of *H. influenzae* with genes of other organisms. In doing so, they were able to predict the purpose of around one thousand genes. The remaining likely had unique functions for the microbe.

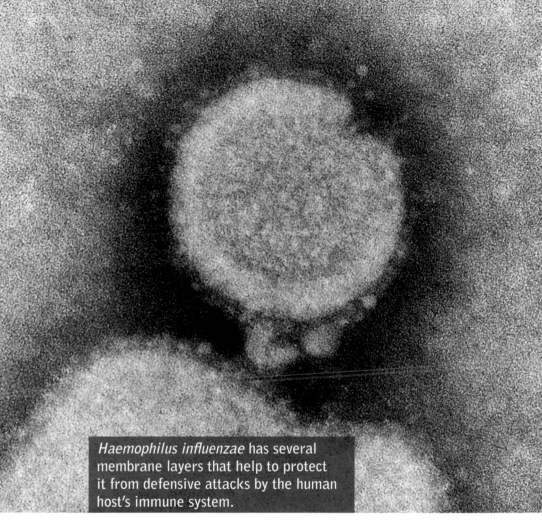

Haemophilus influenzae has several membrane layers that help to protect it from defensive attacks by the human host's immune system.

H. *influenzae* was the first of the Institute for Genomic Research's sequences, but they continued working with several "extremophile" organisms. Extremophiles are organisms that can live in conditions that are typically uninhabitable. They can be found in places with no oxygen, little heat, or even extreme temperatures.

GENETIC DISCRIMINATION BAN

The Americans with Disabilities Act (ADA) became law in 1990. The ADA protects people with physical and mental disabilities. In 1995, the law was updated to include protection for those with genetic disabilities. Genetics and the Human Genome Project were reaching the public. The law now protected people with genes that put them at risk for diseases like cancer. Employers and health insurance companies could not treat someone unfairly based on his or her DNA.

BERMUDA PRINCIPLES

Before proper sequencing could begin, Human Genome Project scientists needed to address how genetic information would be shared. In 1996, a group of international geneticists met in Bermuda. The scientists from the United States, the United Kingdom, France, Germany, and Japan discussed public access to HGP data. They also discussed the **ethics** of gene patenting.

The participants agreed to release sequences longer than one thousand bases to the public each day. They agreed that all sequences should be accessible to the public. They also decided that HGP researchers would not patent any discovered genes.

These agreements, known as the Bermuda Principles, allowed any company or individual to access the project's research. Within four years of the meeting, eleven new disease genes were discovered. The global community had full access to the valuable genetic information.

HUMAN SEQUENCING BEGINS

In April 1996, the Human Genome Project announced the beginning of the most challenging research step yet. The sequencing phase began at six universities in the United States. Each lab first ran a pilot study. Researchers often use pilot studies before starting large-scale experiments. Pilot studies are conducted on a small scale. They allow researchers to evaluate how well an experiment's design will work and how costly the research will be. The HGP pilot studies were to sequence about 3 percent of the total three billion bases by 1998.

Collins explained that the participating universities would also develop and test different ways to sequence DNA. At the time, scientists had several strategies available, but the task of ordering billions of bases required the best genetic technology. The National Institutes of Health and the Department of Energy could then determine the best procedure to use for large-scale sequencing. The six pilot studies would also study smaller, less complex organisms' genomes. This research would help improve sequencing techniques.

The pilot studies took place at six different labs. Dr. Mark Adams and a team at the Institute for Genomic Research sequenced all the genes on chromosome 16. They were also responsible for designing software to store genetic data. Baylor College of Medicine in Houston, Texas, sequenced all the genes of the X chromosome. The Baylor team also developed more accurate sequencing methods.

The Whitehead Institute in Massachusetts focused on improving small-scale sequencing equipment to handle the larger sections of DNA. The machinery needed to work quickly, be inexpensive, and be simple to use. The Whitehead team also focused on sequencing chromosomes 9 and 17. Researchers at Stanford University in California concentrated on improving mapping techniques. They also sequenced parts of chromosomes 4 and 21. The lab at the University of Washington in Seattle was responsible for improving sequencing accuracy. The lab tested these improvements by sequencing parts of chromosome 7.

Lastly, Dr. Robert Waterson and researchers at Missouri's Washington University were at the forefront of sequencing more than thirty-seven million bases in a species of roundworm. The team received praise for their rapid release of information to the public. The Washington University lab was also well known for data organization. During the pilot study, they also tested different organization systems and sequenced parts of chromosomes 22 and X.

INTERNATIONAL EFFORT

The United States was not alone in the sequencing effort. Cooperation between the United States and other countries made the project possible. Research tasks were divided among the international scientific community. The International Human Genome Sequencing Consortium consisted of six countries: Germany, France, Japan, China, the United Kingdom, and the United States. Twenty different universities and labs participated in the six countries.

Many labs in the United States teamed up to work with scientists from other countries. For instance, American and British scientists worked together to sequence other organisms' DNA. Australian scientists contributed to a map of chromosome 16. Japanese scientists assisted in making a map of chromosome 21. Contributions from France were also important to the completion of HGP's mapping goal.

The YEAST SEQUENCE

In 1996, an international team of scientists made an exciting announcement. They successfully sequenced the twelve-million base genome of a species of yeast. Yeast is a single-celled organism important to baking. The effort involved ninety-two different research labs that shared their progress with one another.

This announcement was particularly significant as this was the first eukaryotic genome to be sequenced. Eukaryotes are organisms with cells that contain a nucleus. Humans, along with yeast, belong to the eukaryotic group. The researchers found many genetic similarities between yeast and human genomes. About one-third of the genes found in yeast are similar to those found in humans. Additionally, there are sections in yeast's DNA with identical base order to humans. These matches indicate that these genes probably control the

There are over five hundred different species of yeast. *Saccharomyces cerevisiae*, or brewer's yeast, has been vital in baking, winemaking, and brewing since ancient times.

same cellular processes, like DNA replication and protein synthesis, in both organisms.

In addition to comparisons with human DNA, the sequenced yeast genome assisted scientists in studying gene function. After the announcement, many studies would be conducted in which researchers would stop certain yeast genes from working. Researchers could then observe changes in the organism's traits or behaviors. The yeast genome was also important to early cancer research on the cell cycle.

PARKINSON'S DISEASE

Several National Institutes of Health scientists, working with other labs, discovered the location of the gene responsible for Parkinson's disease. Parkinson's disease gradually affects movement. Over time, symptoms worsen. These symptoms are the result of decline in nerve cell functioning in the brain. There is no cure, but doctors may suggest brain surgery to help control symptoms. Parkinson's disease affects about five hundred thousand people in the United States. Up until the institute's announcement, scientists believed that harmful toxins or drugs caused the disease.

The research team studied the DNA of a family with a high rate of Parkinson's disease. More than sixty members had been diagnosed with the disease. The researchers determined that Parkinson's disease is the result of a point mutation. A single nitrogenous base was substituted for another. The gene, located on chromosome 4, codes for a protein needed for nerve cell functioning. The point mutation can be passed on by the parent to his or her children. Because it is a dominant trait, there is about a 50 percent chance that children will inherit Parkinson's from parents with the mutated gene.

The researchers utilized publically released HGP data to find the gene. Using mapping data, they identified a potential

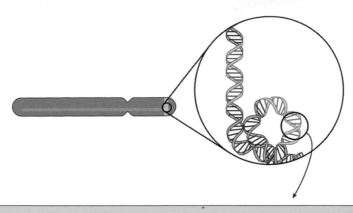

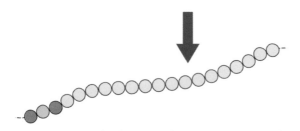

About 15 to 20 percent of people with Parkinson's disease report a close family member with the disease. Scientists have identified mutations involved on several of chromsome 4's genes.

area of about one hundred genes. They were then able to identify the specific gene. Collins praised the finding saying,

Discoveries like this reflect how rapid disease gene identification can be as the Human Genome Project has continued to mine the genome for its treasures. As more gene sites are identified, it will become almost routine for disease gene hunters to find an already characterized gene waiting for them when they arrive at the neighborhood they know is involved in a disease.

A MAP of CHROMOSOME 7

In July 1977, Dr. Eric Green and scientists at the National Human Genome Research Institute finished a complete physical map of chromosome 7. The team spent eight years mapping number 7, which is estimated to contain 5 percent of the total genome. The researchers identified more than two thousand markers on the chromosome. These markers were spaced about every eighty thousand bases out of chromosome 7's 170 million bases. This spacing exceeded the Human Genome Project's goal of markers at every one hundred thousand bases.

Mutations in chromosome 7 are linked to some forms of cancer. Cancer is caused by disruptions to the cell cycle. Alterations in the cycle cause cells to reproduce uncontrollably. These masses of extra cells form tumors, which interfere with healthy organ functioning. Cell cycle disruptions are caused by mutations in a cell's DNA. These mutations can be passed down from parent to child. Depending on the mutation, children may have a higher chance, or be predisposed, to develop certain types of cancers. Other factors can cause changes in a person's genes during his or her lifetime. A substance that can cause mutations is called a mutagen. Cigarettes, radiation, and ultraviolet rays from the sun or tanning beds are examples of mutagens that cause changes to DNA.

Genes on chromosome 7 are believed to play a major role in the regulation of the cell cycle. The map created by Green's team was an important first step in understanding how those genes contribute to the development of cancer.

After announcing the map's completion, the team then partnered with the Washington University pilot study to sequence all the base pairs on chromosome 7.

A NEW FIVE-YEAR PLAN

By 1998, all of the Human Genome Project's five-year goals were completed on schedule. The project had reached the midpoint of its fifteen-year timeline. That year the National

Institutes of Health and the Department of Energy released a new plan to carry the project through 2003. Sequencing would become the primary focus of HGP research. The researchers hoped to complete the entire sequence by 2003, two years ahead of previously set goals.

The 1998 plan had eight objectives. The first goal, a complete sequence of the entire human genome, was an ambitious one. At that point, scientists had only sequenced 6 percent of the genome. The new schedule planned for the completion of the remaining 94 percent in a short five years. To accomplish this goal, an international and US collaboration would continue dividing up portions of the genome and sequencing tasks.

Before they completed the entire sequence, the National Institutes of Health and the Department of Energy planned to release a draft. The draft would include a majority of the sequenced genome but would not be as accurate or complete. They hoped to have at least 90 percent of the genome included in the draft and released by 2001. The following two years would then be about completing the remaining sequences. The researchers would also review the base orders of the final product to ensure accuracy.

HGP researchers would use the 2001 working draft to accomplish the plan's third goal. They would begin researching genetic variation among different research participants. All humans have variations, or differences, in their genes. Most of the differences are single base pairs present in all parts of the genome. Studying those differences would allow scientists to compare and map complex traits and diseases. In addition to comparing variation between humans, the researchers also planned on comparing other species' genetic blueprints with human DNA. To do this, they would sequence several other organisms' genomes. The plan called for these model organism sequences, including the fruit fly and mouse, before the project's completion date in 2003.

Another project goal concentrated on a new area of biology called **functional genomics**. Functional genomics is the study of how genetic data can be used in real world settings. The Human Genome Project also needed techniques and technology to interpret what DNA sequences actually mean. They would also need to develop technology for the enormous amount of sequencing data the project would produce over the next five years.

The new plan also laid out plans for the Ethical, Legal, and Social Implications program. The ELSI would continue to study ethical issues surrounding the project, particularly focusing on health care and society.

Lastly, the 1998 goals focused on connecting genetic research to the public. The Human Genome Project needed to make genetic databases that were easy to use and could be accessed by anyone. The HGP also planned to design more genetic training. As more and more technology was produced, colleges would need to provide training for new geneticists. Medical schools would need to train doctors to use genetic information in their treatments.

CELERA GENOMICS

While the National Institutes of Health and the Department of Energy made the Human Genome Project's sequencing goals public, another organization joined the sequencing effort. Dr. Craig Venter announced that he and another scientist, Michael Hunkapiller, had formed a new business. Venter announced that they would sequence the entire genome in three years.

The new company, Celera Genomics, would use Venter's shotgun sequencing method. It would be much cheaper than the methods used by the National Institutes of Health and the Department of Energy. Venter had used shotgun sequencing to sequence *H. influenzae*. Based on that accomplishment, the scientific community knew that Venter's methods were fast and cost effective. While other organizations worked collaboratively, Celera Genomics began as an independent company. It initially concerned the leaders of the National Institutes of Health and the Department of Energy as they relied on grant funding for their research. They worried that Celera would have more money and would finish first. While Venter and Celera started as competition, they would eventually work with HGP researchers to complete the monumental research effort. Celera's contributions would be crucial to the completion of the project.

The *C. ELEGANS* GENOME

After the pilot studies ended, one of the participating sites, Washington University, began working on model organism sequencing. They partnered with a research institution in the United Kingdom called the Sanger Institute. Their collaboration resulted in the first completely sequenced animal genome. In 1998, the two labs announced that they successfully sequenced a nematode, or roundworm, genome. There are estimated to be more than one million nematode species in the world. Nematodes live in almost every environment and climate. They can inhabit freshwater, salt water, and soil. They are found in both Artic regions and tropical habitats. Nematodes are even present on the ocean floor. More than half of the one million different species are parasitic. Parasites are organisms that live off of another organism. Parasites live on or in the body of another organism, called a host. They provide no benefits to the host and can harm or eventually kill their host. Even if a species of parasite does not cause death, it can still be a source of disease.

The Washington University and Sanger Institute team successfully sequenced the genome of *Caenorhabditis elegans.*

C. elegans is one millimeter long. These nematodes consume bacteria. They also live in multiple environments, particularly in areas with large amounts of decaying plant matter.

The *C. elegans* genome contains ninety-seven million bases. It was an exciting accomplishment as the first single-celled organism's genome had only been sequenced three years prior. *C. elegans*'s genome was much more complex. Their research represented a breakthrough in genetics. Scientists could now compare *C. elegans*'s genome to other organisms' DNA. Dr. Francis Collins was quick to note that about half of the disease causing genes in humans could be identified in the worm.

> I don't think that it is an overstatement to say that the hopes of the parents of a child with a birth defect, the hopes of a young man with a family history of cancer and the hopes of a couple caring for ageing parents are advanced.

The FRUIT FLY GENOME

The year 2000 was full of major achievements for the Human Genome Project. Large-scale sequencing had begun in 1999. In March 2000, an international group of research labs, including Venter's Celera Genomics, completed the sequence of the fruit fly, *Drosophila melanogaster*. The five-year plan released in 1998 originally planned for the fruit fly genome to be sequenced by 2002.

The scientist Thomas Morgan studied fruit fly genes more than fifty years before. Fruit flies had continued to be important in genetic research. Understanding their genetic blueprints meant that scientists could use their DNA to understand how genes work and interact.

"It's a phenomenal milestone," Collins declared, "because of the fruit fly's pivotal role in research, ranging from aging and cancer to learning and memory." Scientists had already determined similarities between the DNA of fruit flies and humans. They also used fruit fly genes to find valuable clues as to how some growth genes work in humans. In fact, they were so important to genetics that three Nobel Prizes had previously been awarded for fruit fly research.

Then, in May 2002, scientists in Japan and Germany announced that all the bases of chromosome 21 had been ordered. Chromosome 21 was the second completely sequenced chromosome. It allowed scientists to being studying the genetic origins of diseases, like Down syndrome and Alzheimer's disease, associated with it.

By June 2000, the Human Genome Project announced that more than 85 percent of the entire human genome was sequenced. The project was on schedule and close to completion.

A DRAFT of the HUMAN GENOME

On February 12, 2001, HGP researchers finished the draft of the human genome. More than 90 percent of the bases were ordered. While there were still some genes that were not complete, the draft advanced scientific knowledge in several critical ways. First, it informed scientists exactly how many genes humans have. At one point, scientists thought that the human genome contained more than one hundred thousand genes. The draft showed that there were between thirty thousand and thirty-five thousand genes. Surprisingly, the draft also indicated that humans only had about twice the number of genes as roundworms or fruit flies. Humans use their genes in clever ways. While genes in other organisms may code for only one protein, human genes may contain instructions for up to three proteins. They also code for more complex proteins than simpler organisms use. The draft also showed that there are many sequences that repeat themselves in the human genome.

Scientists could use these repeating sequences to study the evolutionary history of humans and other species.

The HGP researchers would use the draft to complete the final step of the project, a complete genome sequence with 99.9 percent accuracy and no gaps.

The MOUSE GENOME

The complete genetic blueprint of a mouse was released in 2002 by another collaboration of human genome scientists. The mouse was the first mammal genome to be sequenced. It was also the most similar genome to humans to be released.

The mouse genome is composed of 2.5 billion bases, about .4 billion fewer bases than humans have. Despite a difference in base number, the two species have a similar number of genes but mice do not have as many repeating sequences in their DNA as humans do.

The team of scientists found major differences. The National Institutes of Health explained this by stating that "although virtually all of the human and mouse sequence can be aligned at the level of large chapters, only 40 percent of the mouse and the human sequences can be lined up at the level of sentences and words." These differences indicated shifts in the evolution of mice and humans from a distant common ancestor. Scientists could use the mouse genome to begin studying disease and evolutionary history.

The COMPLETION of the HUMAN GENOME PROJECT

In April 2003, the scientific community celebrated the completion of the Human Genome Project. Dr. Francis Collins declared the project's completion "as more significant than even splitting the atom or going to the moon."

The announcement was made on the fiftieth anniversary of Watson and Crick's discovery of DNA's structure. "Never would I have dreamed in 1953 that my scientific life would encompass the path from DNA's double helix to the 3 billion steps of the human genome," Watson proclaimed.

The final sequence of more than three billion bases was 99.99 percent accurate. The scientific community praised the collaboration between all the scientists and labs that participated in the Human Genome Project. "The international vision and collaboration of the scientists involved played a crucial role in the project's success," said Dr. Mark Walport, a director of one of the HGP labs. "The genome is the common thread that connects us all, so it is only fitting that the sequence has been given to us by scientists from all corners of the earth."

The fully sequenced genome promised advances in medicine and biology. Dr. Eric Lander, another researcher on the project, proclaimed, "The Human Genome Project represents one of the remarkable achievements in the history of science."

Polymerase Chain Reaction

Polymerase chain reaction (PCR) was a vital technology to the Human Genome Project. PCR produces copies of DNA segments in a fast and cheap method. It occurs in a laboratory but essentially models the natural process of DNA replication.

During DNA replication, a specialized protein, the enzyme DNA polymerase, builds the new half of the DNA ladder. It matches new nitrogenous bases with partners on the old strand. For example, if the old strand of DNA has a thymine, DNA polymerase will connect a matching adenine to it.

There are three steps to PCR. First, DNA is placed in a test tube with water. The water is heated, which causes the bonds between base pairs to break. The double helix splits into two strands. PCR makes copies of small sections of the DNA. During the second step, individual indicators, called primers, are attached to the beginning and end of the targeted section. Primers act like traffic lights. They tell DNA polymerase where to start and stop copying during the third stage. After the last step, the process will begin again with both the original and new DNA molecules. During each following cycle, the number of DNA molecules doubles. After twenty cycles, scientists will have more than one million copies, and after thirty, they will have more than one billion.

PCR is controlled by machines that can complete the entire process in a few hours. The Human Genome Project used PCR to produce samples of DNA used for sequencing and mapping.

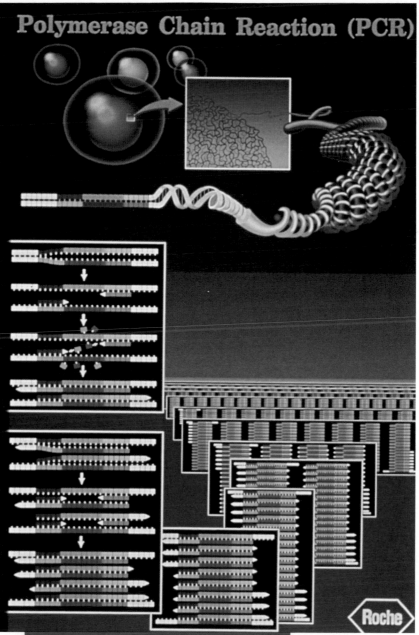

Polymerase Chain Reaction (PCR)

Roche

Called "molecular photocopying," polymerase chain reaction generates multiple copies of a segment of DNA. The creator, Kary B. Mullis, received the Nobel Prize in Chemistry in 1993.

Crops can now be genetically altered to resist pests, survive droughts, and live much closer together in order to produce larger harvests.

CHAPTER 5

The Influence of the Human Genome Project Today

The Human Genome Project concluded in April 2003. Dr. Francis Collins released a report the same month that discussed the future of genomics. Genomics is a field of study within genetics. It is the application of technology, like DNA sequencing and recombinant DNA methods, to study genome functioning. Collins discussed potential scientific discoveries that were possible because of the project.

The report first looked at the effects of genomics on biology. Scientists could now study the function of each individual gene. Having the entire sequence would allow them to study and understand how proteins and phenotypes relate. They could also learn how different cells use genes. This is called gene expression. Understanding the expression of genes would allow geneticists to study all the genomic variations in humans.

Another outcome, Collins wrote, was the impact the Human Genome Project would have on health care and medicine. Doctors now had a complete blueprint to find the cause of diseases. They could locate the genes that help

When Collins and Venter made the announcement that the Human Genome Project was complete, ambassadors from all over the world, including European countries and Japan, attended the ceremony.

individuals fight illness and maintain good health. Medical professionals would be able to develop genetic tests. These tests would identify diseases early on and help develop new treatments. Genomics would influence scientific understanding of traits and human behaviors.

The report went on to discuss the impact of the Human Genome Project on society. A new challenge would be deciding how genetic information should be used. It would be important for scientists to define the appropriate ways for genomics to be utilized. They needed to agree precisely on how genetic information would be shared and who could access that information. Politicians and scientists would have to work together to create laws to protect individuals' rights and regulate genome ownership. Collins wrote that it would also be important to determine guidelines for the medical field and other groups, like schools and the military, that might use genetic information. It would be important to have a general set of rules for all organizations.

Collins concluded the report with an optimistic outlook on the future of genetic research.

Like, Shakespeare, we are inclined to say, "what's past is prologue (*The Tempest*, Act II, Scene 1). If we, like bold architects, can design and build this unprecedented and noble structure, resting on the … foundation of the HGP, then the true promise of genomics research for benefiting humankind can be realized.

FUNCTIONAL GENOMICS and GENETIC ENGINEERING

The field of genomics developed as a result of Human Genome Project advances. Functional genomics examines how genes and proteins work and function together. Scientists in the field of functional genomics work to understand how an organism's genes affect all of its traits. It is important, particularly for the study of genetic diseases, to understand how genes control phenotypes. Scientists can then know what effect mutations might have on an organism.

Another field arose partially from sequencing research. Genetic engineering refers to the ability to remove, add, or change organisms' genomes. Genetic engineering allows scientists to combine different genomes. It also allows doctors to test and treat genetic disorders. Genetic engineering can make exact copies, or clones, of plants and animals, and may even, one day, create artificial life.

GENETICALLY MODIFIED ORGANISMS

Scientists can change an organism's genes to produce certain traits. Organisms with changed genomes are called genetically modified organisms (GMOs). GMO technology takes genes from one species and inserts them into another species' genome.

GMO technology has existed since the early 1980s, when the first genetically modified mice and plants were created. GMOs are heavily used in agriculture. Many plants and animals, like corn, are genetically modified to some extent. Congress first approved genetically modified foods in 1995. By 1999, 50 percent of crops like soybeans, corn, and cotton were genetically modified. Plants are genetically engineered to be stronger. They yield more and are resistant to diseases and pests. For example, a GM plant may have bacteria DNA inserted into its genome that makes it produce chemicals to kill harmful insects. Genetically modified crops also grow faster. Supporters of GM plants point out that they can be used to stop global hunger. Rice, for instance, has been modified to produce higher levels of nutrients and vitamins. GM crops can grow in difficult climates.

Scientists alter the genomes of animals for several reasons. They may include human genes in an animal's genome to study human diseases. Genetically modifying an organism with human genes can also produce materials for medicine. Since the 1980s, scientists have used genetically modified animals to study genetic diseases and test treatments. GMOs can also provide cheaper materials for vaccines and medical drugs.

Scientists also hope that creating GM insects can help prevent parasitic diseases. GM mosquitos, for instance, produce a protein that blocks disease-causing parasites from living in them. The parasite *Plasmodium* causes the disease malaria. Malaria causes flu-like symptoms and can result in death. Without the malaria-causing parasite, mosquitos cannot transmit the disease to humans.

While the first GMOs were established before the beginning of the Human Genome Project, the project's

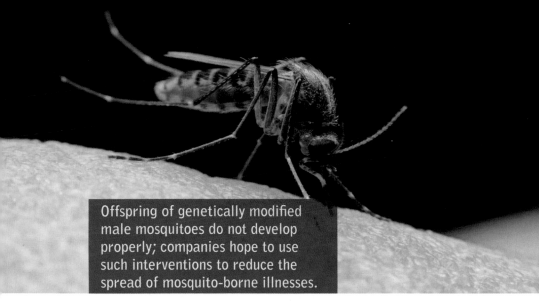

Offspring of genetically modified male mosquitoes do not develop properly; companies hope to use such interventions to reduce the spread of mosquito-borne illnesses.

improvement of sequencing technology expanded the potential uses of GMOs to research diseases and traits.

Controversy surrounds genetically modified organisms. Many countries require the labeling of genetically modified food. However, there are no labeling laws in the United States. While there is a general agreement in the scientific community that GMOs are no more dangerous than normal foods, critics argue that there is not enough evidence of long-term effects on humans. They also point out that GMOs could have adverse impacts on the environment and wild-growing plants.

The HUMAN GENOME PROJECT AT TEN YEARS

Ten years after the Human Genome Project finished, the cures for many genetic disorders were still unknown. However, the project's effects were widespread. In a 2010 issue of *Nature* magazine, writers surveyed a group of biologists. Almost all of them reported being influenced by the Human Genome Project, while 69 percent of the people surveyed said that the HGP helped them decide to become a scientist and 90 percent said that HGP data benefited their research. A major effect of the project, many scientists stated, was the development of new sequencing technology. Dr. Eric Green, the director of the National Human Genome Research Institute, believed that there was still a great deal of research left. He told *Nature*, "While we still don't have all the answers—being a mere 10% of the way into the century with a human genome sequence in hand—we have learned extraordinary things about how the human genome works and how alterations in it confer risk for disease."

GENE THERAPY

Gene therapy uses genes to treat or cure inheritable disorders. Using genetic therapy, scientists can delete, add, or change genes. For example, if a person receives the mutated gene for Huntington's disease, scientists can disable the disease gene using genetic therapy. Mutated genes can also be replaced by healthy ones. Gene therapy may also introduce new genes into the body to fight diseases.

As researchers involved in the Human Genome Project raced toward the finish line in the late 1990s, a genetic scandal was unfolding in another geneticist's lab. In 1999, gene therapy was a new area of biomedical research. One of the most prominent scientists at the time, Dr. James Wilson, worked at the University of Pennsylvania's Institute for Human Gene Therapy. Wilson and his team conducted experiments to find the cure for a rare disorder using gene therapy. The disease, called OTCD, causes blood poisoning in patients when they consume certain foods. Wilson and his team hoped to cure OTCD by inserting a working gene in place of a mutation. They used viruses to deliver the gene to a cell's nucleus. There the gene was combined with the cell's DNA. Wilson first developed this method of viral delivery in the early 1990s. It was successfully used to treat liver disorders in both experimental animal and human trials. However, his OTCD research took a tragic turn. One of the patients became very ill and died from the viral delivery method. Essentially, his immune system rejected the foreign body and caused him to sicken very quickly. As a result, Wilson was no longer able to conduct research. The government banned Wilson from working on human trials for five years. Along with Wilson's personal consequences, gene therapy research stopped. Experiments peaked in 1999 during Wilson's OTCD work, but by 2001, there were only thirty-four ongoing gene therapy trials. In recent years, Wilson has resumed gene therapy research. He relies on the same method of viral delivery but is carefully studying the effects that it can have on different people's immune systems.

The completion of the Human Genome Project, the creation of new DNA technology, and Wilson's new research has reopened the doors for genetic therapy research. In fact, the potential for gene therapy has expanded since HGP completion. As new technology increases the speed with which scientists can genetically alter traits, gene therapy may one day become as common as prescribing medication or performing surgery to treat diseases. As of now, it is only being tested on genetic disorders and other diseases that have no cure. Researchers must ensure that the method is safe before use in the general public.

CANCER RESEARCH

Gene therapy can fix problems in the human genome. It can even enhance genetic characteristics. For instance, gene therapy can be used to attack cancer cells. Genes that code for special proteins that attack cancer are inserted into immune system cells. The cells can then target cancer cells and kill them.

In 1971, the US government declared a "war on cancer." Dr. Renato Dulbecco, one of the early supporters of the Human Genome Project, voiced the necessity of a complete human sequence to understand the genetic origins of tumors and cancer.

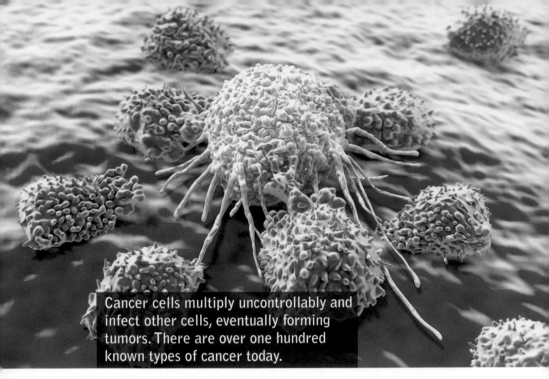

Cancer cells multiply uncontrollably and infect other cells, eventually forming tumors. There are over one hundred known types of cancer today.

Since the project's completion in 2003, cancer research has been able to rapidly expand. Prior to 2003, scientists understood the basics of cancer and the role of a few genes. The completed human genome sequence provided researchers with reference genes that could be compared and studied. Almost immediately after the HGP's final publication, researchers found 291 genes associated with cancer. They then turned to creating an entire record of all the mutations related to a particular disease or found in a specific individual. Using the human genome sequence, cancer researchers began to use whole-genome sequencing, or WGS, to produce an entire genome sequence at one time. WGS is not yet widespread in genetic research, but it lends valuable information on cancer mutations.

From this initial research, multiple projects have been created. The Cancer Genome Atlas, the Cancer Genome Project, and the International Cancer Genome Consortium are all organizations focused on cataloging all the mutations of many adult and childhood cancers.

Created three years after the completion of the Human Genome Project, the Cancer Genome Atlas (TCGA) is an effort of two divisions of the National Institutes of Health, the same labs involved with the HGP. The mission of the TCGA is to create an "atlas" or genetic map of all the mutations involved in cancer. It began as a pilot study in 2006 and ended in January 2015. The project uncovered information on multiple types of cancer and created genetic profiles of more than ten thousand tumors. Scientists are now debating the next steps. Some wish to continue sequencing and others are more focused on the functional genomics of cancer genes.

GENETIC COUNSELING

The medical field has benefited from genome research in many ways. Individuals can be tested for genetic disorders. Doctors can also predict how likely it is that a child will be born with a genetic disorder if a particular disease runs in a family.

Prenatal Diagnosis

Prenatal tests are given to test for blood type, health conditions, and genetic abnormalities of unborn babies. They can be given before or after a woman becomes pregnant. Prenatal tests can identify treatable health problems. They can also be used to test for genetic problems. Prenatal tests can be either screening tests or diagnostic tests. Screening tests can only determine the possibility that a child will be born with inherited disorders. Diagnostic tests identify specific issues. The tests analyze specific genes of the parents.

Individuals who want to have children but may be at risk for genetic problems can be tested. Tests are also given if there is a family history of a particular inherited disease. The risk of some chromosomal mutations, like Down syndrome, increase with the mother's age. Older mothers can also be tested for such disorders. Some genetic mutations occur with higher frequencies in certain ethnic groups. Individuals belonging to those groups may opt to be tested before having children.

While someone may not have a genetic disorder, he or she could be a potential carrier of the disease trait. The human genome sequence allowed doctors to compare different human genomes so they can examine genetic variation to make a diagnosis.

DESIGNER BABIES

With a complete blueprint of the human genome, doctors can test, or screen, individuals for genetic disorders. New technology may also make it possible to change non-disease-related genes. In 2013, Dr. Tony Perry announced that he successfully edited mouse DNA. To edit DNA means to change genes or single bases in an organism. The ability to alter DNA would allow parents to replace genes for disorders like cystic fibrosis or sickle-cell anemia. However, this technology has the potential to change more than just mutated genes. Even before Perry's announcement, there was already a large debate in the scientific community over "designer babies."

Parents may soon be able to choose traits for their unborn children using editing technology. Editing DNA would allow the modification of features like hair or eye color. Some people worry that such technology would be harmful to society. At a summit in Washington, D.C., in 2015, chairperson David Baltimore and other geneticists gathered to discuss the question of "when, if ever, we will want to use gene editing to change inheritance." Some scientists are confident that gene selection will be a reality in the future. Dr. Ronald Green, a professor at Dartmouth College and author of *Babies by Design: The Ethics of Genetic Choice*, believes that modifying genes will not only be used to treat disorders. He argues that parents may select certain traits, like height or intelligence, for their children.

CRISPR

Genetic modification is possible through technology like CRISPR. CRISPR is a method of gene editing that can quickly and cheaply change an organism's genome. The CRISPR editing technique naturally occurs in organisms like bacteria. Bacteria use CRISPR to defend themselves against viruses and other invaders. With CRISPR, bacteria can cut sections of their DNA. Scientists can use this biological technology to cut and edit genes in plants and animals. Genes can be added or removed. Any edits made using CRISPR can be inherited by an organism's offspring. Scientists began using the procedure in 2011. It has been used to make mosquitos immune to a harmful disease-causing parasite, create miniature pigs, and stop cancer cell division.

Genetics is not yet capable of changing complex traits. CRISPR can be used to edit simple traits, but scientists do not entirely understand traits that result from multiple gene interactions, like intelligence or artistic talent.

However, CRISPR promises advances in gene therapy. If scientists can edit genes quickly and efficiently, they can easily target mutated genes. In fact, the editing tool has been used to treat adult mice with Duchenne muscular dystrophy. DMD is a genetic disorder characterized by the progressive decline of muscles. Muscle weakness begins as early as three years old. The disease primarily affects boys, as it is sex-linked, or caused by a mutation on the X chromosome. About one in five thousand babies is born with DMD. The genetic mutation prohibits the production of a protein responsible for connecting muscle fibers and tissues.

Although rare, it can also occur in girls if two copies of the recessive mutation are inherited. Until recently, sufferers of DMD did not survive past adolescence. With advanced medical treatments, individuals with DMD live longer, even into their forties and fifties. Using CRISPR, scientists delivered the gene editing system to muscle cells using a new virus delivery

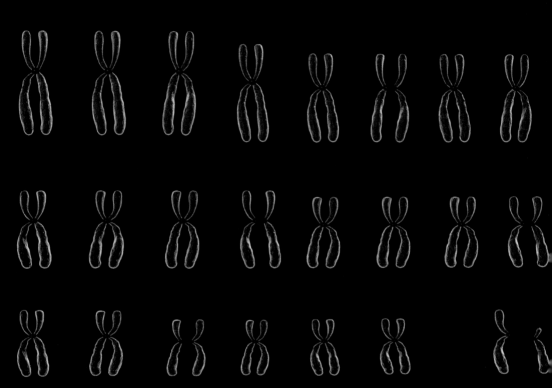

First observed in the mid-nineteenth century, the identification and display of chromosomes provides important genetic information.

method pioneered by James Wilson after his initial gene therapy research. Scientists injected a mouse with the virus's regular copies of the gene. CRISPR then cut out the defective gene. The use of gene therapy via CRISPR in humans will take many more studies. Scientists must understand how to direct viruses to particular cells before attempting the experimental method in humans. CRISPR-directed gene therapy will be a promising cure. "There is still a significant amount of work to do to translate this to a human therapy and demonstrate safety. But these results coming from our first experiments are very exciting. From here, we'll be [improving] the delivery system, evaluating the approach in more severe models of DMD, and assessing … safety in larger animals," said Charles Garsbech, a biomedical engineer at Duke University.

KARYOTYPING and PEDIGREES

Scientists can test for chromosomal mutations using a special genetic testing tool called a karyotype. A karyotype is a photographic display of an individual's paired and numbered chromosomes. To create a karyotype, scientists grow an individual's cells in a lab. The cells are photographed during mitosis. Chromosomes condense during this phase of the cell cycle and are much easier to see. The chromosomes are stained and sorted and then displayed. Each chromosome has about four hundred visible bands. Each band contains hundreds of genes.

Karyotypes allow scientists to visibly see chromosome mutations. For instance, a karyotype of an individual with Down syndrome would have three chromosome 21s. These tests can be performed on individuals to provide a diagnosis or to predict the likelihood of the mutation occurring again.

Scientists may also use a tool called a pedigree. Pedigrees use special symbols to trace the prevalence of a genetic disorder within a family. They are primarily used to both record family genetic history and to predict outcomes for future generations.

GENETIC TESTING

Identifying genetic problems is not limited to karyotypes or pedigrees. Genetic testing can locate specific gene mutations and diagnose diseases. Genetic tests can also identify the risk of disease for people or their children. There are several types of genetic testing for different purposes.

Diagnostic testing identifies a genetic disease that is making an individual ill. Another type of test, predictive, is used to find genetic mutations that may increase a person's chance of becoming ill. Predictive tests, for example, can be used to detect a person's risk for developing certain types of cancer. Carrier testing determines if a person has a mutated gene for a particular disorder. That person can pass on mutated genes to his or her children. Carrier testing is useful for individuals who have a family history of genetic disease. It may also be helpful for those who belong to ethnic groups that are at higher risk for specific illnesses. Medical testing evaluates how a person's body reacts to certain treatments. There are no known physical risks to genetic testing; however, experts worry about the potential emotional and financial costs of testing. Geneticists or genetic counselors may guide families through the complex issues that surround genetic testing.

Genetic tests are given in a medical setting; however, direct-to-consumer, or at-home, genetic tests allow individuals to receive genetic information without the input of a doctor. Companies send genetic tests to the participant's home, and the participant collects a sample of saliva from his or her cheek. The saliva contains a DNA sample. The participant then mails the sample to a laboratory. Results are mailed or posted online. At-home genetic testing varies in cost. An advantage is providing participants with valuable genetic information. Experts caution that results may be misleading without the help of a medical professional to interpret them. They also worry about the unofficial release of individuals' genetic information.

When considering genetic testing, it is important to remember that while genes accurately predict genetic problems, other factors may influence outcomes. Lifestyle choices, diet, and environmental factors may lessen or increase the risk of many disorders.

NEXT GENERATION SEQUENCING

Sequencing technology is rapidly changing. By 2014, sequencing machines produced one thousand times the amount of data that a machine in 2005 could. The Human Genome Project took fifteen years to complete and cost billions of dollars. Current technology can sequence more than forty-five genomes in a single day for about $1000. Around eighteen thousand different genomes can be sequenced in a year.

Whole genome sequencing produces complete sets of genomes. The method is useful for identifying disease genes. While better than earlier sequencing techniques, WGS is not the fastest method. It sequences every gene, both those that code for proteins and those that do not.

Exome sequencing is an alternative sequencing method. The exome refers to only the protein-coding genes. It composes a very small percentage of the human genome but contains most of the disease-causing genes. Exome sequencing is useful for studying diseases.

Targeted sequencing identifies specific parts of the genome. Researchers use targeted sequencing to focus their experiments. It allows them to identify rare mutations that might be missed using larger-scale sequencing.

The field of genetics also now includes the study of epigenetics. Genes may be switched on or off by external factors. Epigenomics studies how cells read genes. Scientists who study epigenetics examine how cells control gene function instead of differences in genes. Factors like proteins may change certain genes without changing the nitrogenous bases. Genetic researchers hope that new sequencing technology will explain complex diseases like autism or depression.

ARTIFICIAL GENOME SYNTHESIS

The leaps in genetic discoveries since the Human Genome Project include the relatively new process of creating synthetic, or artificial, genes in a lab. Artificial genome sequencing (AGS) does not need an original DNA sequence. Instead, scientists can create original genomes with unique base sequences. AGS differs from cloning, which produces identical copies of an organism's genome.

One of the pioneers in the field of AGS is Dr. Craig Venter, the former head of Celera Genomics, which contributed to the completion of the sequenced human genome. In the early stages of sequencing technology, bases were recorded and converted into an electronic code. Computer databases store the information. Venter and a research team at the J. Craig Venter Research Institute wanted to reverse the process. They wanted to know if they could start with a digital code that would produce nitrogenous bases and, when combined, an entire genome.

In 2003, they first successfully created, or synthesized, a virus. In 2008, they built a small bacteria genome. While impressive, the two artificial genomes did not work. The cell did not carry out life processes and did not produce proteins like naturally occurring DNA.

The year 2010 marked a breakthrough in artificial genome sequencing. The research team created a 1.08 billion-base synthetic bacteria genome. Not only was the entire genome unique, but the cell was also self-replicating, meaning that the cell can divide and produce new cells on its own. The genome was generated using a computer. Laboratory machines then combined the necessary chemicals to make base pairs and the other parts of a nucleotide.

The genome was then placed into the empty nucleus of a cell. The DNA was transcribed into mRNA and proteins were produced. After a few days, the scientists observed growing numbers of cells in the lab sample. The cells were replicating and passing on their synthetic DNA to their daughter cells. The ultimate goal of Venter's team is to create an entire cell from scratch to understand how cells function. By creating the smallest genome possible, the researchers hope to understand how essential genes work.

NEXT STEPS

The field of genetics is always changing and evolving. Since the conclusion of the Human Genome Project in 2003, researchers have created genetic therapy, developed testing procedures, and even created a synthetic genome.

Now, researchers look toward the future of genetic research and medicine. "What I'd like to do is have your genome done as a starting point in medicine," Venter said in 2014. He believes that to do this, scientists must sequence as many different people's genomes as possible. "One genome is basically worthless," Venter said at a Future of Genomic Medicine meeting. "Without something to compare it with, you can't interpret it. A hundred doesn't get you much better. We need 500,000 to a million genomes." Scientists can use sequenced genomes to personalize medical treatments. Venter recently partnered with a research laboratory at the University of California, San Diego, to sequence cancer patients' genomes and tumor genes. Doctors could use this information to one day stop the expression of mutated cancer genes.

In a January 2016 blog post, Dr. Francis Collins praised the scientific accomplishments of 2015. Collins expressed hope for the future of genetics and medicine.

> Given how swiftly the field of medicine is moving, it is impossible to predict where we might stand in 25 years, let alone 125 years. However, one thing is certain: From my vantage point at the helm of the

world's leading supporter of biomedical research, I see a broad horizon filled with exciting opportunities—many with the potential to transform medicine.

The Human Genome Project paved the way for incredible advances in how we understand the way living things work. From Gregor Mendel's experiments with pea plants to James Watson and Francis Crick's discovery of the structure of DNA, the Human Genome Project was the realization of many years of dedicated scientific study. The future of genetics and medicine will continue to change, as our genetic code is further understood and decoded.

The Ethics of Genetic Engineering

Bioethics is the study of ethical issues surrounding scientific and medical developments. While genetic engineering is transforming medicine, many scientists and bioethicists are cautious of the new technology and genetic manipulation. They argue that as new technology is made, the scientific community and the public must consider the long-term effects of such advances. Dr. Paul Root Wolpe, a bioethicist, cautioned the audience of a talk he gave about bioethics.

> We are now taking control of our own evolution. We are directly designing the future of the species of this planet. It confers upon us an enormous responsibility that is not just the responsibility of the scientists and the ethicists who are thinking about it and writing about it now. It is the responsibility of everybody because it will determine what kind of planet and what kind of bodies we will have in the future.

The personalization of medicine through genetics is near, and with it come many ethical questions that must be answered. Gene therapy and testing, designer babies, and artificial genomes all have the potential to treat and one day cure genetic disorders and other genetically linked diseases. The Human Genome Project raised remaining bioethical questions. Who owns genetic information? How should genomic information be stored and shared? How far should scientists go in changing and controlling DNA? These questions and other ethical concerns must be addressed even as genetics is on the edge of revolutionary change.

Chronology

1865	Gregor Mendel publishes the results of his pea plant genetic experiments
1869	Frederich Miescher identifies DNA, or nuclein, within a cell nucleus
1905	Punnett, Saunders, and Bateson identify the linkage of genes
1911	Thomas Morgan establishes the Fly Room at Columbia University
1920	Alfred Sturtevant publishes the first genetic map
1949	Edward Chargaff conducts experiments indicating equal amounts of nitrogenous bases
1952	Rosalind Franklin creates DNA photograph that indicates a double-stranded structure; Linus Pauling propose a triple helix model
1953	James Watson and Francis Crick discover the structure of DNA

1959   Jerome Lejeune and colleagues discover the cause of Down syndrome

1961   Marshall Nirenberg discovers the process of protein synthesis

1973   Herbert Boyer and Stanley Cohen develop recombinant DNA technology

1977   Frederick Sanger develops DNA sequencing method

1983   Huntington's disease is genetically mapped; polymerase chain reaction technique is developed

1989   Mutation that causes cystic fibrosis identified

1990   The Human Genome Project begins

1993   Dr. Francis Collins is appointed head of the Human Genome Project

1995   The Haemophilus influenzae genome is sequenced

1996   The Bermuda Principles are drafted for genome access; yeast genome is sequenced

1998   Celera Genomics is founded; Human Genome Project releases new five-year plan; C. elegans genome is sequenced

1999 Chromosome 22 becomes first sequenced human chromosome

2000 Fruit fly genome is sequenced

2001 Working draft of the Human Genome Project is finished

2002 Mouse genome is sequenced

2003 The Human Genome Project is completed

Glossary

allele Any of the alternative forms of a gene that may occur at a given locus.

autosome A chromosome other than a sex chromosome.

bioethics A discipline dealing with the ethical implications of biological research and applications especially in medicine.

cell cycle The complete series of events from one cell division to the next.

chromosome The part of a cell that contains the genes that control how an animal or plant grows and what it becomes.

deoxyribonucleic acid A substance that carries genetic information in the cells of plants and animals.

dominant Causing or relating to a characteristic or condition that a child will have if one of the child's parents has it.

double helix The structural arrangement of DNA in space that consists of paired polynucleotide strands stabilized by cross-links between purine and pyrimidine bases.

ethics An area of study that deals with ideas about what is good and bad behavior; a branch of philosophy dealing with what is morally right or wrong.

functional genomics A branch of genomics that uses various techniques to analyze the function of genes and the proteins they produce.

gene A specific sequence of nucleotides in DNA or RNA that is located usually on a chromosome.

gene map A diagram showing the relative locations of each known gene on a particular chromosome.

gene therapy A way of treating some disorders and diseases that usually involves replacing bad copies of genes with other genes.

genetics A branch of biology that deals with the heredity and variation of organisms.

genome The genetic material of an organism.

genotype All or part of the genetic constitution of an individual or group.

heredity The sum of the characteristics and potentialities genetically derived from one's ancestors.

heterozygous Having two different alleles for a single trait.

homozygous Having two identical alleles for a single trait.

incomplete dominance The property of being expressed or inherited as a semidominant gene or trait.

inheritance All of the genetic characteristics or qualities transmitted from parent to offspring.

meiosis The cellular process that results in the number of chromosomes in gamete-producing cells being reduced to one-half.

mitosis A process that takes place in the nucleus of a dividing cell; involves typically a series of steps consisting of prophase, metaphase, anaphase, and telophase; and results in the formation of two new nuclei, each having the same number of chromosomes of the parent nucleus.

multiple allele An allele of a genetic locus having more than two allelic forms within a population.

mutation A relatively permanent change in hereditary material.

nitrogenous base A nitrogen-containing molecule with basic properties; especially one that is a purine pyrimidine.

nucleotide Any of several compounds that consist of a ribose or deoxyribose sugar joined to a purine or pyrimidine base and to a phosphate group and that are the basic structural units of RNA and DNA.

nucleus A cellular organelle of eukaryotes that is essential to cell functions.

phenotype The observable properties of an organism that are produced by the interaction of the genotype and the environment.

protein A macromolecule that contains carbon, hydrogen, oxygen, and nitrogen; needed by the body for growth and repair and to make up enzymes.

Punnett square A diagram showing the gene combinations that might result from a genetic cross.

recessive Causing or relating to a characteristic or condition that a child will have if both of the child's parents have it.

replication The copying process by which a cell duplicates its DNA.

ribonucleic acid A substance in the cells of plants and animals that helps proteins.

sex chromosome A chromosome that is inherited differently in the two sexes.

Further Information

WEBSITES

DNA Timeline
www.dnai.org/timeline/

The DNA Learning Center website features a timeline of all genetic research and scientists from the pre-1920s until 2000.

National Human Genome Research Institute:
National DNA Day
www.genome.gov/10506367

Collection of educational resources on the Human Genome Project and National DNA Day.

Unlocking Life's Code Timeline
www.unlockinglifescode.org

An online exhibit on genetic discoveries and information on the Human Genome Project compiled by the Smithsonian National Museum of Natural History in partnership with the National Human Genome Research Institute.

BOOKS

Ridley, Matt. *Genome: The Autobiography of a Species in 23 Chapters*. New York, NY: Harper Perennial, 2006.

Schultz, Mark. *The Stuff of Life: A Graphic Guide to Genetics and DNA*. New York, NY: Hill and Wang, 2009.

VIDEOS

"We Can Now Edit Our DNA. But Let's Do It Wisely."
www.ted.com/talks/jennifer_doudna_we_can_now_edit_our_dna_but_let_s_do_it_wisely/transcript?language=en

In this TED talk video, Jennifer Doudna discusses how CRISPR DNA editing works and ethical issues associated with the new technology.

"Welcome to the Genomic Revolution"
www.ted.com/talks/richard_resnick_welcome_to_the_genomic_revolution?language=en

In this TED talk video, Richard Resnick discusses how genetic technology is used in medicine today and how it may be used in the future.

Bibliography

Academy of Achievement Staff. "Interview: Francis Collins."
    Retrieved December 5, 2015 (http://www.achievement.org/
    autodoc/printmember/col1int-1).

Angier, Natalie. "Great 15-Year Project to Decipher Genes
    Stirs Opposition." *New York Times*, June 5, 1009. Retrieved
    November 30, 2015 (http://www.nytimes.com/ 1990/06/05/
    science/great-15-year-project-to-decipher-genes-
    stirsoopposition.html).

Christensen, Jen. "In Vitro to Gene Editing: Slow Crawl to
    Designer Babies." CNN News, December 3, 2015. Retrieved
    December 18, 2015 (http://www.cnn.com/2015/12/ 03/
    health/designer-babies-gene-editing).

Collins, Francis, Eric Green, et. al. "A Vision for the Future
    of Genomics Research." *Nature*, 422 (2003). Retrieved
    December 13, 2015.

Collins, Francis. "Francis Collins Says Medicine in the
    Future Will Be Tailored to Your Genes." Retrieved January
    5, 2016 (http://www.wsj.com/articles/francis-collins-
    says-medicine-in-the-future-will-be-tailored-to-your-
    genes-1404763139).

Collins, Francis. "Happy New Year…and a Look Back at a Memorable 2015." Retrieved January 5, 2016 (http://directorsblog.nih.gov/2016/01/05/happy-new-year-and-a-look-back-at-a-memorable-2015/#more-5637).

DNA Learning Center Staff. "The Central Dogma." Retrieved November 17, 2015 (http://www.dnalc.org/view/15876-The-Central-Dogma.html).

DNA Learning Center Staff. "Edwin Chargaff, 1950." Retrieved November 20, 2015 (http://www.dnalc.org/view/16012-Erwin-Chargaff-1950.html).

DNA Learning Center Staff. "Linus Pauling Triple Helix Model." Retrieved November 17, 2015 (http://www.dnalc.org/view/15512-Linus-Pauling-s-triple-DNA-helix-model-3D-animation-with-basic-narration.html).

Dockrill, Peter. "CRISPR Gene Editing Tool Used to Treat Genetic Disease in an Animal for the First Time." Retrieved December 30, 2015 (http://www.sciencealert.com/crispr-gene-editing-tool-used-to-treat-genetic-disease-in-an-animal-for-the-first-time).

Gallagher, James. "'Designer Babies' Debate Should Start, Scientists Say." BBC News, January 19, 2015 Retrieved December 15, 2015 (http://www.bbc.com/news/health-30742774).

Genetics Home Reference. "What Is Gene Therapy?" Retrieved December 20, 2015 (http://ghr.nlm.nih.gov/handbook/therapy/genetherapy).

Genetics Home Reference. "What Is Genetic Testing?"
Retrieved January 2, 2016 (http://ghr.nlm.nih.gov/
handbook/testing/directtoconsumer).

Genetics Home Reference. "What Were Some of the Ethical,
Legal, and Social Implications Addressed by the Human
Genome Project?" Retrieved December 18, 2015 (http://ghr.
nlm.nih.gov/handbook/hgp/elsi).

Genome.gov. "A Brief History of the Human Genome Project."
Retrieved November 11, 2015 (http://www.genome.
gov/12011239).

Genome.gov. "All About the Human Genome Project."
Retrieved November 11, 2015 (http://www.genome.
gov/10001772).

Genome.gov. "About NGHRI: A Brief History and Timeline."
Retrieved November 11, 2015 (http://www.genome.
gov/10001763).

Genome.gov. "Genetic Timeline." Retrieved November
11, 2015 (http://www.genome.gov/Pages/Education/
GeneticTimeline.pdf).

How Stuff Works.com. "Alfred H. Sturtevant." Retrieved
December 10, 2015 (http://science.howstuffworks.com/
dictionary/famous-scientists/biologists/alfred-h-sturtevant-
info.htm).

J. Craig Venter Institute. "J. Craig Venter." Retrieved December 4, 2015 (http://www.jcvi.org/cms/about/bios/jcventer/).

Mallet, Jim. "The Peppered Moth: A Black and White Story After All." *Genetics Society News*, no. 50 (2003): 34–38.

McElheny, Victor K. *Drawing the Map of Life: Inside the Human Genome Project*. New York: Basic Books, 2010.

Miller, Kenneth R., and Joseph S. Levine. "Unit 4 Genetics." *Prentice Hall Biology*. Upper Saddle River, NJ: Prentice Hall, 2004.

Muscular Dystrophy Association. "Duchenne Muscular Dystrophy." Retrieved December 30, 2015 (http://www.mda.org/disease/duchenne-muscular-dystrophy/overview).

National Human Genome Research Institute. "The Cancer Genome Atlas." Retrieved Dec 26, 2015 (http://www.genome.gov/17516564).

National Institutes of Health. "Deciphering the Genetic Code: Marshall Nirenberg." Retrieved November 18, 2015 (https://history.nih.gov/exhibits/nirenberg/).

National Center for Biotechnology Information. "J. Craig Venter." Retrieved December 4, 2015 (http://www.ncbi.nlm.nih.gov/pmc/articles/PMC3068906/).

National Down Syndrome Socieity.org. "What Is Down Syndrome?" Retrieved November 27, 2015 (http://www. ndss.org/Down-Syndrome/What-Is-Down-Syndrome/).

National Library of Medicine. "The Rosalind Franklin Papers: Biographical Information." Retrieved November 17, 2015 (https://profiles.nlm.nih.gov/ps/retrieve/Narrative/KR/p-nid/183).

Nature Education. "Thomas Hunt Morgan: The Fruit Fly Scientist." Retrieved November 11, 2015 (http://www. nature.com/scitable/topicpage/thomas-hunt-morgan-the-fruit-fly-scientist-6579789).

Nobelprize.org. "Frederick Sanger." Retrieved November 30, 2015 (http://www.nobelprize.org/nobel_prizes/chemistry/laureates/1958/sanger-bio.html).

Office of NIH History. "Gregor Mendel: The Father of Genetics." Retrieved November 11, 2015 (https://history. nih.gov/exhibits/nirenberg/HS1_mendel.htm).

San Diego Supercomputer Center. "Rosalind Elsie Franklin." Retrieved November 17, 2015 (http://www.sdsc.edu/ ScienceWomen/franklin.html).

Stanford Children's Health. "Structural Abnormalities: Deletions and Duplications." Retrieved Nov 28, 2015 (http:// www.stanfordchildrens.org/en/topic/default?id=str uctural-abnormalities-deletions-cri-du-chat-and-duplications-pallister-killian-90-P02147).

US Department of Energy. "About the Human Genome Project." Retrieved November 14, 2015 (http://www.omi.gov/hgmis).

UShistory.org. "The Manhattan Project." Retrieved November 22, 2015 (http://www.ushistory.org/us/51f.asp).

Waddingham, Anne, comp. *The Britannica Guide to Genetics.* Philadelphia: Running Press Book Publishers, 2009.

Wolpe, Paul Root. "It's Time to Question Genetic Engineering." Filmed November 2010. TED video, 19:42. Posted March 2011 (http://www.ted.com/talks/paul_root_wolpe_it_s_time_to_question_bio_engineering?language=en).

Index

cystic fibrosis, 43, 61, 98
cytokinesis, 31, 32
cytosine, 19, 21, 22, 29, 39, **51**

defensive proteins, 22
DeLisi, Charles, 56
deoxyribonucleic acid
    (DNA), **8**, 15, **20**, 22, 23,
    45, 49–50, 61, **87**
    discovery of, 13
    and Human Genome
        Project, 66–74, 76–106
    mutations, 25, 26, 37–40,
        44, 55
    and radiation, 25, 26, 55
    replication, 30–31, 32, 33,
        37–38, 51, 52
    sequencing, 23–24, 50–52,
        54, 55, 56, 58, **59**–60
    structure, 17, 19–21, 24, 27,
        29, 56, 85
diploid number, 32
DNA helicase, 31, 39
DNA polymerase, 31, 86
Dolly, **4**–6, 7
dominant, 12, 14, 33, 34, 35,
    36, 42, 43
double helix, 19, 21, 30–31,
    47
Down syndrome, **41**–42, 44,
    45, 83, 97, 101
Dulbecco, Renato, 55

ethics, 72

frameshift mutations, 40
Franklin, Rosalind, 17–**18**, 19,
    24, 27
functional genomics, 80, 91
fruit fly, **14**, **15**, 32, 33, 48, 60,
    79, 82–83

genes, 15, 16, 21, 33, 42, 43,
    61, 62
    and determination of
        organism type, 17,
        24
    gene mapping, 16, 26,
        44, 47, 48–**49**, 50, 54,
        69–106
    gene therapy, 7, 94–95,
        99–101, 107
    linkage, 48
genetically modified
    organisms, 6–7 , **88**,
    92–**93**, 98, 107
genetic disorders, caused by
    mutation, 40–44
genetics
    counseling, 97–98
    Mendelian, 33–35
    what it is, 6, 13
genome, what it is, 44
genotype, 35, 43
guanine, 19, 21, 22, 29, 39, **51**

Haemophilus influenza,
    70–**71**, 80
haploid number, 33

hemophilia, 44
heredity
  and Mendel, 12, 15
  and Morgan, 15
heterozygous, 35, 43
homozygous, 34, 43
Human Genome Project, 26,
  47, 51, 54, 55, 56, 65–66,
  86
  and cancer research, 78
  collaboration with Celera,
    80–81
  completion of, 7, 84–85
  and discrimination, 71–72
  ethical concerns, 66–69
  first animal genome
    sequencing, 81–82
  first draft of human
    genome, 83–84
  five-year plan
    first, 65–66
    second, 78–80
  future of research since
    project completion,
    105–106
  influence of, 89–105
  international collaboration,
    74
  making a complete genetic
    map, 69–70
  profiles of leaders of, 57–62
  sharing of research, 72,
    76–77
  start of sequencing, 72–74

Huntington's disease, 43, 54,
  62, 94
hybrid animals, 6

incomplete dominance, 36
inheritance
  and Mendel, 10, 12, 32,
    33–35, 48
  and Morgan, 13–15
Institute for Genomic
  Research, 59–60, 70, 71, 73
interphase, 31

karyotyping, 101
Klinefelter syndrome, 42

Lacks, Henrietta, 67
law of dominance, 12, 15
law of independent
  assortment, 12
law of segregation, 12, 15

Manhattan Project, 25
Marfan syndrome, 43
McClintock, Barbara, 16–17
meiosis, 33, 40–41, 48
Mendel, Gregor, 7, 10, 24, 32,
  44, 47, 106
  genetics, 33–35
  laws of heredity, 12–13, 32,
    33, 48
    alternatives to, 35–37
Mendelian inheritance, and
  genetic disorders, 42–44

Miescher, Frederich, 13, 15, 24

mitosis, 31–32, 45

Morgan, Thomas, 13–15, 16, 24, 32, 47, 48, 82

mouse genome, sequencing of, 60, 79, 84

mutations, **26**, 37–38, **39**, 45, 50, 91

    genetic disorders caused by, 25, 40–44, 76, 94

    positive, 25, 38

    types of, 38–40, 55, 78, 96, 97, 98, 101

National Institutes of Health, 23

nematodes, **64**, 81–82

Nirenberg, Marshall, 22, 24

nitrogenous base, 19, 21, 22, 23, 24, 25, 27, 29, 31, 40, 47, 49, 50, 52, 103

nucleic acid, 29, 37

nucleotide, 19, 21, 24, 27, 29, 37, 38, 39

nucleus, 13, 29, 30, 94

Painter, Theophilus, 45

Pallister Killian disorder, 42

Parkinson's disease, 76–77

Pauling, Linus, 27

pea plants, 10, 13, 33, 34, 34, 44, 48 106

phenotype, 33, 38

point mutations, 38–40, 43, 76

polymerase chain reaction, 86, **87**

proteins, 23, 24, 25, 51, 68

    synthesis, 22–23, 29, 39, 40

    what they are, 21–22

Punnett square, 33, **34**, 35, 48

purines, 19, 21, 29

pyrimidines, 19, 21, 29, 30

radiation, 25

recessive, 12, 14, 33, 34, 35, 36, 37, 42, 43, 44

recombinant DNA, 49–50

ribonucleic acid (RNA), 22, 23, 24, 29–30, 61

Saccharomyces cerevisiae (brewer's yeast), **76**

Sanger, Frederick, 23–24, 51–**53**, 54, 60, 66

shotgun sequencing, 60, 70, 80–81

sickle cell disease, 25, 43–44, 98

Sinsheimer, Robert, 55

stem cell research, 6

structural proteins, 22

Sturtevant, Alfred, 16, 48–49, 50

thymine, 19, 21, 23, 29, 30, 43, **51**

About the Author

Megan Mitchell is a Teach For America alumna and former biology educator. She attended the University of Texas, where she worked as a research assistant in the Children's Research Lab. She has written many lesson plans for her classroom and designed middle school science curriculum. Mitchell is currently a graduate student at the University of California, Davis. She loves gardening, hiking, reading, and performing scientific experiments. She hopes that one day genetics will be able to explain why her two dogs, Butters and Toast, have such silly personalities.